Acclaim for
Ludmilla Petrushevskaya

"Petrushevskaya writes instant classics."
—*The Daily Beast*

"Petrushevskaya is the Tolstoy of the communal kitchen. . . . She is not, like Tolstoy, writing of war, or, like Dostoyevsky, writing of criminals on the street, or, like poet Anna Akhmatova or novelist Aleksandr Solzhenitsyn, noting the extreme suffering of those sent to the camps. Rather, she is bearing witness to the fight to survive the everyday. . . . [She is] dazzlingly talented and deeply empathetic."
—*Slate*

"This celebrated Russian author is so disquieting that long after Solzhenitsyn had been published in the Soviet Union, her fiction was banned—even though nothing about it screams 'political' or 'dissident' or anything else. It just screams."
—*Elle*

"Her suspenseful writing calls to mind the creepiness of Poe and the psychological acuity (and sly irony) of Chekhov."
—*More*

"Petrushevskaya's fiction [offers] a glimpse of what it means to be a human being, living sometimes in bitter misery, sometimes in unexpected grace."
—Jenny Offill, *The New York Times Book Review*

PENGUIN BOOKS

The Girl from the Metropol Hotel

Ludmilla Petrushevskaya was born in 1938 in Moscow, where she still lives. She is the author of more than fifteen volumes of prose, including the *New York Times* bestseller *There Once Lived a Woman Who Tried to Kill Her Neighbor's Baby: Scary Fairy Tales*, which won a World Fantasy Award and was one of *New York* magazine's Ten Best Books of the Year and one of NPR's Five Best Works of Foreign Fiction; *There Once Lived a Girl Who Seduced Her Sister's Husband, and He Hanged Himself: Love Stories*; and *There Once Lived a Mother Who Loved Her Children, Until They Moved Back In: Three Novellas About Family*. A singular force in modern Russian fiction, she is also a playwright whose work has been staged by leading theater companies all over the world. In 2002 she received Russia's most prestigious prize, The Triumph, for lifetime achievement.

Anna Summers is the coeditor and cotranslator of Ludmilla Petrushevskaya's *There Once Lived a Woman Who Tried to Kill Her Neighbor's Baby: Scary Fairy Tales* as well as the editor and translator of Petrushevskaya's *There Once Lived a Girl Who Seduced Her Sister's Husband, and He Hanged Himself: Love Stories* and *There Once Lived a Mother Who Loved Her Children, Until They Moved Back In: Three Novellas About Family*. Born in Moscow, she now lives in Cambridge, Massachusetts.

Also by Ludmilla Petrushevskaya

There Once Lived a Woman Who Tried to Kill
Her Neighbor's Baby: Scary Fairy Tales

There Once Lived a Girl Who Seduced Her Sister's Husband,
and He Hanged Himself: Love Stories

There Once Lived a Mother Who Loved Her Children,
Until They Moved Back In: Three Novellas About Family

The Girl from the Metropol Hotel

Growing Up in Communist Russia

LUDMILLA PETRUSHEVSKAYA

Translated with an Introduction by Anna Summers

PENGUIN BOOKS

PENGUIN BOOKS

An imprint of Penguin Random House LLC
375 Hudson Street
New York, New York 10014
penguin.com

Originally published in Russian by Amfora, St. Petersburg, 2006.

Image credits: pp. xv, xviii, 46, 86: Wikimedia Commons; p. xvii: still from *The Fable of Fables* by permission of Soyuzmultfilm Studios; p. 12: photo by Arkady Shaikeht, January 1942, from waralbum.ru; p. 14: photo by Semyon Fridliand, October 1941, from waralbum.ru; pp. 17, 23, 38: photographer unknown, from www.waralbum.ru; p. 27: "Slow spring in Strukovsky Garden," by Vladimir Kleschev, 2012. Used with permission of the photographer; pp. 68, 98: From pastvu.com; p. 120: *Moscow Courtyard* by Sergei Vokov, used with permission by the artist.
All other images courtesy of the author.

Published with the support of the Institute for Literary Translation (Russia)

LIBRARY OF CONGRESS CATALOGING-IN-PUBLICATION DATA
Names: Petrushevskaëiìa, Lëiìudmila, author.
Title: The girl from the Metropol Hotel : growing up in communist Russia / Ludmilla Petrushevskaya ; translated with an introduction by Anna Summers.
Other titles: Malen§kaëiìa devochka iz "Metropolëiìa". English
Description: New York, New York : Penguin Books, [2017] | Original Russian edition: 2006.
Identifiers: LCCN 2016031256 (print) | LCCN 2016035280 (ebook) | ISBN 9780143129974 (paperback) | ISBN 9781101993514 (ebook)
Subjects: LCSH: Petrushevskaëiìa, Lëiìudmila—Childhood and youth. | Petrushevskaëiìa, Lëiìudmila—Family. | Petrushevskaëiìa, Lëiìudmila—Friends and associates. | Authors, Russian—20th century—Biography. | Moscow (Russia)—Biography. | Hotel Metropol (Moscow, Russia)—History—20th century. | Moscow (Russia)—Social life and customs—20th century. | Communism—Social aspects—Soviet Union—History. | Coming of age—Soviet Union. | Soviet Union—History—1925–1953—Biography. | BISAC: BIOGRAPHY & AUTOBIOGRAPHY / Personal Memoirs. | BIOGRAPHY & AUTOBIOGRAPHY / Literary. | HISTORY / Europe / Russia & the Former Soviet Union.
Classification: LCC PG3485.E724 Z4613 2017 (print) | LCC PG3485.E724 (ebook) | DDC 891.78/4403 [B]—dc23
LC record available at https://lccn.loc.gov/2016031256

Printed in the United States of America
5   7   9   10   8   6   4

Set in Adobe Calson • Designed by Patrice Sheridan

This translation is dedicated to my father,

Arnold Friedrich, another wartime orphan,

and to George Scialabba,

an author, editor, and friend.

Contents

Introduction

Ludmilla Petrushevskaya's War

Every year on May 9, old men all over Russia—in every village and town, no matter how small or squalid—don their best suits, attach medals to their lapels, and shuffle outside to participate in street "parades." The old men, generally neglected by a state uninterested in its citizens, especially in the decrepit among them, have this one day on which they are honored and extolled.

That's how it used to be. In 2015, on the seventieth anniversary of the end of World War II, no rows of veterans paraded through city or village streets. Instead, for the first time, portraits of the veterans were carried by their grandchildren, who marched to the same war-themed music that has filled Russian airwaves every May for decades. The veterans, frail and stooped, in their old-fashioned berets and oversize Sunday suits sporting rows of medals, are dead—save for a bare handful. So are their wives and the more numerous war widows. That incredible generation is gone, and the war that was part of Russia's consciousness every day for seventy-five years has finally receded. The veterans' great-grandchildren, today's teenagers, are the first generation for whom the Great Patriotic War isn't living reality but just another historical fact.

The war hasn't disappeared entirely, though. Before today's teens came two other generations, for whom the war remains a living memory: the veterans' children, like Ludmilla Petrushevskaya, who are now in their seventies, and their grandchildren, who are now in their thirties and forties. The younger of these, like me, born thirty years after the war, are connected to it by our direct link with the veterans, the old men and women who shared our little apartments and homes, raised us, cared for us, were our beloved *dedushka*s and *babushka*s. Every family in every part of the enormous country, without exception, shared wartime experiences through their grandparents. Those experiences were a commonplace subject as early as kindergarten, where the first question between toddlers was, "What did your grandpa do in the war?" A proud or mournful answer followed, facts were exchanged, ice broken.

Except sometimes the facts of a family's connection with the war weren't suited for proud retelling and were therefore often concealed from the little ones, who would then be forced to hem and haw and finally come up with some lie. Sometimes our grandparents didn't just die gruesomely, burning alive in a tank, like mine, or return disfigured, or even return at all. Sometimes they were arrested and sent to the Gulag, like Solzhenitsyn's Ivan Denisovich and Solzhenitsyn himself, for some imaginary wrongdoing at the front, or, even more inconveniently, arrested en masse and executed before the war had even begun, like Petrushevskaya's. In a scene in the memoir, Petrushevskaya is mortified when other wartime toddlers boast about their fathers and uncles fighting at the front and she can't come up with a single name. Thirty years later, I would be mortified, too.

．　．　．

The arrest and execution of Petrushevskaya's relatives—prominent Bolsheviks elevated by the October Revolution—in the late thirties ensured, among other things, that *her* war would be different from the war of her peers. The shared experiences of their childhoods—evacuation, hunger—were heightened in her case to an unbearable—and unshareable—extreme because of the social stigma that branded her an "enemy of the people." That was the official status of Petrushevskaya's remaining family throughout her childhood. And, she points out wryly, it was no joke. At a time when everyone was cold, dirty, and hungry, she and her aunt and grandmother, who until recently had resided in great comfort at the Metropol Hotel, were hungrier, dirtier, and colder than everyone else. They were banned from the shared bathroom in their communal apartment; in the endless food lines, they were always the last to be served; police wouldn't protect them when neighbors attacked them, even with an ax; and they were open prey to any thug—and this in a town full of bandits. Most important, those men at the front weren't fighting for *them*. They were everyone's enemies, from the soldier at the front to the janitor in their apartment building. The Great War that temporarily equalized Russia's population, turning it into a brotherhood and sisterhood of suffering, extended no welcoming hand to little Petrushevskaya and her wretched aunt and grandmother. Though they were eventually all rehabilitated, during the war they were interned like Japanese Americans during the same period, except their camp had invisible walls and they were the only ones in it.

All this makes Petrushevskaya's memoir unique, and potentially gruesome. Yet there is nothing gruesome about it. From heartrending facts Petrushevskaya concocts a humorous and lyrical account of the toughest childhood and youth imaginable. The child in her book, like all children, has been endowed with gifts from two fairies, an evil one and a kind one. The evil fairy, a definite heavyweight, took away the child's home, her mother, her father, her clothes, her toys, her food, and her civil rights, leaving her without shoes in wintertime. The kind fairy, doing what she could, gave the child excellent health, mental resilience, a hunger for beauty and culture, an unerring ethical compass, and an array of talents. A faithfully observed balance between deprivation and fullness, physical scarcity and inner abundance, social scorn and artistic triumph, lifts Petrushevskaya's account above self-pity and places it alongside the classic stories of humanity's beloved plucky child heroes: Édith Piaf, Charlie Chaplin, the Artful Dodger, Gavroche, David Copperfield. Petrushevskaya's girl is right up there, dancing a gypsy dance at an orphanage, singing her heart out in the school choir despite having nowhere to live, reading herself blind at the public library after school, ignoring hunger cramps, and, much later in life, writing her incomparable prose "into the desk," unpublishable and unpublished. The child is irresistible and so is the adult narrator who creates a poignant portrait from the rags and riches of her memory.

● ● ●

The Metropol Hotel is a vast art deco building in downtown Moscow, steps away from Red Square, where the country's main Victory Day parades take place. Today it is once again a world-class luxury hotel. The lobby and the bar are empty in the day-time. The only visitors are listless women in miniskirts and sheer pantyhose, with peroxide hair and provincial faces. They are to-day's "girls from the Metropol," as prostitutes are sometimes called in everyday Muscovite slang. "Why are you dressed like a girl from the Metropol?" a shocked mom may ask her daughter. Petrushevskaya and her young mother were also called "girls

The Metropol Hotel today.

from the Metropol," but with a very different meaning. After the
October Revolution the famed building was designated the Second House of Soviets. For many years it housed the Party government and prominent revolutionaries, like the author's
great-grandfather. To reside in that building was like having a
mailing address at Buckingham Palace. Hence the double meaning of Petrushevskaya's title. From a Bolshevik princess, the girl
from the Metropol descended to Moscow's nether regions occupied by prostitutes, beggars, and the homeless. She left the
Metropol a pampered toddler and returned there at the age of
nine, a wild, lice-ridden, emaciated Mowgli. Naturally she and her
poor mother weren't allowed to stay in that exalted, orderly establishment. Their wanderings and social alienation continued.

What would have happened if she had stayed? If, miraculously,
she had found refuge in the building that symbolized the new re-
gime and housed the new elite? If on May 9, the girl had proudly
crossed Revolution Square in front of the Metropol and joined the
Victory Day parade, watching the men in medals with different eyes,
as someone for whom they had officially fought and shed blood? If
she had never known such scorn, such helplessness, such hunger and
cold, never run barefoot or sung on street corners for food? Then we
would have no Petrushevskaya—and we, selfishly, would regret it.
The art that shines so brightly in this little book was born not in a
palatial hotel among Party bosses but on Kuibyshev's dirty streets, in
view of the majestic Volga River, and under Petrushevskaya's grandfather's dinner table, where she and her mother found shelter of sorts
when they were turned away from the Metropol. And now, every
year on May 9, Russian state television shows an animated film, *The
Fable of Fables* (also translated as *Tale of Tales*) (*Skazka skazok*), writ-

Still from *The Fable of Fables* (1979), directed by Yuri Norstein, art by Franchesca Yarbusova.

ten by Petrushevskaya. A national and international sensation when it came out in 1979, the film tells the story of a little wolf cub, abandoned in wartime, who is a reincarnation of the memoir's street urchin, the little girl who survived the war.

The book begins with the author's earliest memories and ends with her coming of age, when she finishes college and begins her first job as a journalist. It is composed as a series of vignettes that allows full-screen glimpses of her life in different periods. Petrushevskaya is famously reticent and rarely grants interviews. *The Girl from the Metropol Hotel* was her first volume of autobiography, ardently welcomed by her fans. When the book came out in 2006, it received the prestigious Bunin Prize—fittingly, since its art is undoubtedly Buninesque. These two masters, like no others, understand how to collect squalid facts, reassemble them, and present the resulting fable in such a way that the reader sees mostly art and beauty, with filth and hard-

Majolica mosaic *La Princesse lointaine* (1896–1905), by Mikhail Vrubel.

ship confined to the corners of one's eyes, to the narrative's unlit margins. Suddenly the evil fairy's gifts appear unimportant and irrelevant, and the book's foreground is occupied by very different memories: a golden autumnal tree, a piece of Tchaikovsky's music, a stained glass window, a favorite teacher, a sunrise over the steppe. And the reader is gripped by a desire to hug this little girl, to pull her close, to tell her that it was for her, for her incredible talent, for her future art, that our grandfathers died in the war, that she just has to wait, to hang on, and the disgusting fog of lies that have caused her so much suffering will dissipate like the clouds on the famous Vrubel mosaic that adorns her beloved Metropol.

ANNA SUMMERS

The Girl from the Metropol Hotel

The Girl from the Metropol Hotel

When we leave this life, our memories and accumulated knowledge leave with us, but some traits and habits may be passed on to the next generation. Extreme, often unreasonable stubbornness; a conviction that food must be spartan (despite unbridled gluttony during holidays) and showers cold; indiscriminate hatred for the authorities; loyalty to one's principles, even if one's family must suffer; a sentimental fondness for music and poetry and unseemly squabbling over trifles; a fierce honesty in all affairs and utter disregard for deadlines; love for humanity and acute hatred for the next-door neighbor; need for both silence and constant screaming; the ability to survive on nothing most of the time and then mad spending on presents; a terrible mess in the house, while insisting on everyone else's cleanliness; and endless love for the little ones, especially when they are asleep in all their cherubic beauty.

* * *

My great-grandmother Asya died from sepsis at thirty-seven, leaving six children. Her husband, Ilya, walked down to the river to drown himself—he was a doctor and held himself responsible. The five children ran after him, carrying the baby; they stopped him on the riverbank. When Asya was being buried, one daughter, Valentina, my future grandmother, trailed her father like a shadow, mumbling, "I'll always follow in your steps."

And she did—she became a revolutionary, a member of an underground cell, just like he was. An erstwhile defender of the oppressed, he worked among the poor all his life, usually as a

The Veger family on a stroll in 1912. My grandmother Valentina is in a white blouse. Behind her, my great-grandfather Ilya Veger (Dedya) and grandfather Nikolai Yakovlev. Dedya disliked when his daughters got married. That probably explains his belligerent expression.

doctor at some factory, treating all the sick from the surrounding villages. He never accepted money for his services, living only on his salary. He would see every patient, as a matter of principle, although he was paid to treat only the factory personnel. He was regularly fired and would usually find his next job in an area struck by some epidemic, like cholera, where all medics who applied were hired, even the ones with a criminal record.

As soon as I could talk, I called him "Dedya."

Family Circumstances.
The Vegers

I was born in Moscow's most famed residential building—the Metropol Hotel. It was also called the Second House of Soviets, because its rooms were occupied by the Old Bolsheviks, such as my great-grandfather Dedya—Ilya Sergeevich Veger—a member of the Russian Social-Democratic Workers' Party since 1898. In the same building, after her divorce, lived his daughter, my grandmother Valentina, a Bolshevik since 1912, with her two daughters: my aunt Vava and my mother, also Valentina.

All three, as it happens in fairy tales, were wonderful beauties. My grandmother had been courted by the young poet Vladimir Mayakovsky; Vava, with her dark blue eyes, long braid, and snowy smile, was the prettiest student in the Armored Transport Academy; my mother, who was tall for her age, attracted attention early on, especially from soldiers, and innocently answered their questions about her name and address (though not her age—fourteen), which greatly upset her mother and older sister. A hardworking student, she consumed mountains of books (she was majoring in literary studies) and took literature so seriously that simple reading for pleasure she considered a sacrilege. Secretly, she was in love with the portrait of young Maxim Gorky. And this naïve, serious-minded, and completely innocent girl became pregnant on her twenty-first birthday, on August 23, 1937. As a child, I heard her say laughingly to our heavily pregnant janitor, Granya, that to her "it" happened the very first time—and she pointed at me.

During the summer of that cursed year, my future family lived in Silver Forest, Moscow's summerhouse area. (The house belonged to my grandmother's older brother Vladimir, an Old Bolshevik, the

Valentina ("Liulia") and Vera ("Vava"), my mother and aunt, in 1930. That year my mother and grandmother ran into the poet Vladimir Mayakovsky on the trolley bus. The poet seemed exhausted and gloomy. He committed suicide months later.

leader of the underground revolutionary cell in Moscow and one of the organizers of the 1905 uprising. In Vladimir's house a young Mayakovsky fell in love with my grandmother; Vladimir was the one who inducted the poet into the Bolshevik party.) In May, my grandmother's younger brother Zhenya, two sisters, Asya and Lena, and their spouses, all prominent Bolsheviks, were arrested and, with the exception of Asya, never seen again. Their official sentence was "ten years of hard labor without the right to correspondence"—a euphemism for the firing squad.

My grandmother was left to wait her turn. Every night she heard the gate open and footsteps rustle on the gravel. But nobody came to arrest her. She couldn't sleep and went to see a psychiatrist, who told her to stay at the clinic, where she would be safe. She did, and this probably saved her life—they were arresting everyone except for certified psychotics. When the young wife of her arrested brother lost her mind from nightly interrogations, they let her go. (Her end was terrible: she, her mother, and her little son were buried alive, along with other Ukrainian Jews, by the advancing Nazis.)

But my grandmother was completely healthy. Stefan, my future father, visited my mother at the dacha that summer. It was Stefan's footsteps that my grandmother must have heard, when he tiptoed over the gravel to my mother's window, to summon her outside—such is my theory. He went to the same college as my mother, majoring in philosophy, while my mother studied literature. Later that fall, at a general meeting of students and faculty, my mother's case was discussed and Stefan disowned us (my mother and me, in her belly), because we were relatives of the arrested enemies of the people. Another student, a consumptive boy, my mother's admirer, stood up and offered to marry her if my father was refusing! Later my father changed his mind and married her after all, though not for long.

Approximately two years after these events, upon coming home to their apartment at the Metropol, my grandmother and her daughters found their doors sealed by the Party's own police and intelligence agency (NKVD). My grandmother began to open one, then stopped, turned on her heel, and walked away without a word. Aunt Vava, who followed her out, saw that the door handles were encircled with a wire, and on the wire hung a lead seal. If they had returned an hour earlier they would have been taken. But my family is always late. With nothing—clothes, utensils, bedding, books, not to mention furniture and paintings, all remained in the sealed apartment—they knocked on Dedya's door in the same building and took up residence in his room. But I do retain a fragile memory of my first home: two adjacent rooms and over the connecting door an exquisite portrait—my maternal great-grandmother. That portrait, long vanished in NKVD's underground storages and probably appropriated by one of "theirs," marked the beginning of my life; that is, my memory.

Other earliest recollections:

. . . I'm learning how to walk—taking unsteady little steps along the couch, holding on to the seat. I'm practicing on a summerhouse porch—it's flooded with the evening sun. I'm squinting happily against the sun rays. I learned to walk late, after a prolonged pneumonia. I'm happy, I'm having fun, and Mama is happy that I can finally walk. Happiness is associated with warmth, light, green foliage, and Mama. This is 1939.

. . . The Metropol Hotel. I'm standing in the middle of an

enormous room, in front of the connecting doors and my grand-mother's portrait—a swan neck, burgundy hair. I hear someone shout that I be careful and not to step into the full potty.

. . . I fall from a trunk on which I was sleeping. A dark, narrow room, piled with furniture and luggage. I split my head. I see tall, concerned people, their long shadows. This isn't our suite in the Metropol. This is somebody else's house. Our own apartment there has been sealed, and now we are "wandering"— an important word from my childhood vocabulary. I still have a scar on my left temple.

.   .   .

The Metropol Hotel. Postcard from 1905.

I was born on May 26, 1938, nine months after my mother's twenty-first birthday. I was lucky. I wasn't left behind in a sealed apartment, as often happened to the infants of the arrested. I grew up by my grandmother's side, to the sound of Russian classics—but more on this later.

The War

M y uninterrupted memories begin with the war, summer of 1941. Mama is carrying me to a bomb shelter, a designated subway station after hours. I'm watching the night sky, criss-crossed by light beams; they look like fireworks. In reality, they are plane detectors. I remember not wanting to go underground, stretching my neck toward the festive sky, demanding to stay and watch the lights. But down we go, and spend the night on sheets of plywood laid over the tracks. My mother always carried with her a bag with blankets. I can see the arched ceiling of the black tunnel—it's an adventure!

In October 1941, Dedya, my grandmother Valya, my mother and I, and my aunt left Moscow for Kuibyshev (Samara before and after the Soviet Union) in a cattle car. According to my aunt, people were forced to evacuate, especially children and the elderly.

My aunt went to the station to see our train. It consisted of shiny new trolleys, mounted on wheels, and at the very end a

Women and children taking cover in the Moscow subway during a bomb alert in 1942.

cattle car, very dirty, with a thick layer of what looked like chalk all over the floor. My aunt knew that enemies of the people like us would not be put on a clean new bus, so she immediately proceeded to sweep the cattle car. The next day my mother joined her, and for many hours they scrubbed, using pieces of plywood as shovels. When everything was clean, they brought the rest of us: Dedya, my grandmother, and me, and also our luggage, which consisted mainly of blankets. The weather was extremely cold; it was the beginning of the terrible winter of 1941. My family spread one blanket over the floor, covered themselves with the rest, and sat like this for several days, waiting for the train to depart. At the last moment, they were joined by the train's officer in charge, with his wife and child. He must have realized that the metal trolleys were virtual iceboxes and wisely chose our cattle car, though it, too, was freezing.

We were lucky he did: At the very first stop he resourcefully procured a small cast-iron furnace that looked like a barrel with a chimney. He had noticed neat rows of coal along the tracks, for the train's engine. During stops, the grown-ups jumped off the car and gathered up the coal to feed our furnace. As a result, it was almost warm, and there were two kettles bubbling cozily. (That feeling of coziness, of home, when a match strikes and a tiny circle of light appears, always returned when I had to settle in a new place. Never have I been frightened by circumstances. A little warmth, a little bread, my little ones with me, and life begins, happiness begins.)

I remember living inside Dedya's coyote coat, watching the fire in the furnace through the crack. Dedya spent that journey like a kangaroo, letting me out only occasionally.

October 1941. Moscow outskirts; defense lines.

At night, the train would halt in the steppe, letting Moscow-bound military trains pass. They carried fresh troops from Siberia, well fed, well dressed, and well armed. Moscow's own defenders had no rifles or winter coats; they were clerks, factory workers, and high school students, and they were dying en masse among the frozen summerhouses. The authorities had no time to think about them and were preparing to give up the city. In November it was already snowing. The terrible winter was upon us.

I was let off the train to stretch my legs in the snowbanks along the tracks. I remember that at one stop my mother fed me "pastry"—a slice of white bread. I had a poor appetite and was thought to have TB like my father and so many others in Moscow. But at that moment, looking out over the white horizon under the black sky, I must have felt something, some foreboding of the coming hunger, and licked up every crumb.

Kuibyshev

At one of the stops, Dedya handed me over to the women, walked out on the platform, and disappeared. He boarded a faster passenger train, to get there first and find housing, like a quartermaster arriving ahead of the troops.

In Kuibyshev, as an Old Bolshevik and civil war hero, he was assigned a separate hotel room. By the time we reached Kuibyshev, Dedya had found us all housing: a narrow shoe box with two beds and a small table. Dedya and I slept in one bed, and my grandmother with two daughters in the other, with extra chairs for their feet.

Despite these conditions, Dedya took a cold bath every day (with a bowl of water and a rag) and performed Müller exercises. My grandmother, his daughter, hardly left the bed: the result of a contusion she'd sustained during a terrorist bombing at the Moscow Party Committee.

The Moscow government offices also evacuated to Kuibyshev. The Bolshoi Theatre came, followed by the Durov Theatre of Animals. A munitions plant arrived, too. My mother was sent to work there in the packaging department; Aunt Vava, an engineer who hadn't finished her degree, also found work. Mama moonlighted reading poetry to the wounded soldiers and also wrote about art for the local paper. One of her subjects was a huge canvas that adorned the waiting room of Kuibyshev's train station: a fascist soldier dying alone in the winter steppe, watched over by a gray wolf. This shocking artifact I remember in the greatest detail, having spent many hours staring at it during our later "wanderings." My mother wrote a long article about it.

Eventually Dedya moved us to a communal apartment in a residential building for army officers, where the four of us occupied two rooms connected by a door. Even though three of his children had been sentenced for political crimes, Dedya still commanded the respect of Party members and received some assistance. Devoted colleagues and pupils brought him gifts of food; I even remember a bunch of grapes on a saucer. I spent a lot of time in Dedya's room; he fed me and took care of me. But he had to return to Moscow, and at the same time my mother received a letter of acceptance from the revived Institute of Theatre Arts, also in Moscow.

It was a miracle. My mother had left the Literary Institute after the memorable general college meeting, while she was pregnant with me, but it is possible that she was never officially expelled. She didn't mention any of it in her application, didn't mention her executed relatives, enemies of the people; she just put down four years of studies and was accepted. (Until the sixties, when Stalinism was partially condemned, she concealed the truth about her family, disliked talking about the past, and

Women evacuees at work at one of Kuibyshev's wartime factories.

avoided mentioning "political repressions." During her last year, when she couldn't leave her bed, I suggested to her, "Let's try to remember happy times," but she only moved her fingers, as if brushing something away.)

Still, there were some bright moments—that acceptance letter, for example. My mother was passionate about studying; her dream was to finish college. On receiving the letter, she tried to obtain a train ticket to Moscow, but that was impossible. Train tickets didn't exist in wartime.

She even asked our neighbor Rahil, the horror of my childhood, for help, because her husband worked for the railway. Rahil herself told me this decades later, when I was visiting Samara with my play and found our old apartment. Rahil still lived in her room, alone. I informed her that my aunt and grandmother had been rehabilitated, and that my mother had died, but that Vava, my aunt, lived in a private apartment in the center of Moscow and received a state pension. Solemnly, Rahil explained to the curious neighbors who'd gathered to listen to us that during the war she'd had to hide all the foodstuffs from us, had to keep everything under lock. "But I was five, I was starving—we had nothing to eat," I said and broke into tears. The neighbors' eyes bulged: not to give a crumb to a starving child! Rahil quickly retreated to her room, an impoverished, ancient hag.

My mother left by sheer accident. On the way home from the store, she detoured to the station to look at the departing Moscow train, walked up to the drivers, and, without any hope, asked for a lift, as she often did. And the drivers agreed! They let her stand on the engine; she wasn't allowed in the cabin. All she had with her was a bottle of cooking oil and a week's salary, which she gave to the drivers. There was no time to run home, and she was probably afraid, too. I don't know if it was a freight train or a passenger train; a freight train could easily take a week.

What was she thinking of, standing for days on the exposed engine in her sundress? Most likely she was thinking of me. She probably tried to convince herself that I would be okay, that she was leaving me with her mother and sister, that I was in day care, and that we would manage somehow. She needed to get her diploma, first and foremost, and then bring me to live with her.

I imagine how her heart must have pounded when the train started moving. She was going to Moscow, to study! She was twenty-seven years old.

On arriving in Moscow, she settled in her father's room in a communal apartment on Chekhov Street. The room was crowded with bookcases. She lived under the dinner table. Immediately she sent us a letter and a money transfer: she had managed to obtain child support from my father, her former husband. She wore her father's old army coat over the sundress to classes. She had no other clothes.

Back in Kuibyshev, her mother and sister accepted her disappearance without much joy. Her name was never mentioned again. On the other hand, so many people had vanished from their lives. At that time it was common—people disappeared without a trace, like the character in Daniil Kharms's famous poem about a man who walked out of his house and was never seen again. Later, the poet himself vanished.

I waited for my mother day and night. She returned four years later.

She used to tell me again and again that it was for me, for my sake, that she left, that she couldn't have supported us without a college degree. For the rest of her life my poor mother justified herself.

Kuibyshev.

Survival Strategies

There we were, the three of us: my grandmother, my aunt, and me. Aunt Vava was fired from her job at the munitions plant after an all-night interrogation. She was a dangerous element: her relatives had been executed as enemies of the people. We lived on what my mother sent us: my child support, courtesy of my father, a young philosophy professor.

Then real hunger set in.

During the war, one could purchase food only with ration cards. We received rations for one child and two dependents. With ration cards we bought black bread. With each purchase, the store cut out coupons from our cards. Long before the end of the month, all our bread would be "cut out."

The bread line formed early, before dawn, among the pillowy snowdrifts. It ended in front of the heavy white metal door. The rule "Whoever's last in line, I'll get behind you" saved lives in the chaos of wartime. Clinging to the person ahead of us, we found ourselves in the realm of order and justice, with a nominal right to survive. People guarded their spots with their lives, ready to shed blood if someone tried to jump the line. In those days one couldn't step away "for just a moment."

After hours of waiting, we were inside the little store, where it was warm. The smell of bread was dizzying; it made our jaws ache and stomachs churn. Hunger was consuming our insides, forcing us to stretch our necks and take mincing steps from side to side, to create an illusion of progress. The thick line swayed without moving.

Finally, our turn came. The weight of the loaf was always less than the regulation stipulated, and the saleswoman dropped an extra piece that made the metal scale go down for a split second—and immediately the bread was taken off the scale. It was the simplest racket. Still, that extra piece was valued immensely and usually went to the child. I swallowed mine on the spot. The rest of the bread we divided "fairly" into three parts. I gobbled down mine the same night, breaking little pieces under the pillow. Then my aunt and grandmother would feed me their shares. Later, when I asked my aunt how we survived, she shrugged and smiled bewilderedly. "I don't know . . ."

I attended day care for a short while. There, the underage population lived its own life. We ate glue in secret because of the rumor that it was flavored with real cherries—we dipped our fingers in the jar during arts and crafts and licked them. We also believed that the witch Baba Yaga resided in the hallway, as the custodian wanted us to believe, especially after she mopped the floors. Then there was a ritual: when a military plane passed overhead, we were expected to look up solemnly and name a family member fighting on the front, as though it was him flying on that plane. It was a matter of pride, but I couldn't name anyone. Humiliated, I demanded names from my aunt. She thought long and hard; all the men in our family had been shot or jailed, if you didn't count my consumptive father. Still, she scraped up two names. From then on I proudly announced, "There's my uncle Volodya (or Uncle Serezha) flying!" I didn't know who they were. Later I learned that mysterious Volodya was my aunt's ex-husband, and Serezha turned out to be my own great-uncle! He was only seventeen years older than me. (I met him sixty years later at the family banquet to celebrate the 140th anniversary of Dedya's birth. Serezha was his youngest son, fathered with his third wife when Dedya was in his fifties. And he actually was a pilot during the war.)

But I had to stop going to the day care: we couldn't pay, and there was the problem of shoes. In the north, the lack of shoes for the poor was the biggest hardship. In the villages, peasants made shoes from tree bark, but we lived in the city. From April to October I ran barefoot—from last snow to first. No one mentioned TB anymore—I never even had a runny nose.

Wartime kindergarten.

How I
Was Rescued

There was a whole pack of us children, and we spent our days on the Volga River. I didn't know how to swim, but that wasn't necessary: our bank was shallow and descended gently. When spring came and the Volga flooded, though, my clumsiness and irresponsibility nearly cost me my life.

In May, the Volga flooded to the size of an ocean. Our bank was completely underwater; the opposite shore was barely visible. Together with another little girl, I decided to explore that mysterious side, so we squirreled our way onto the ferry and crossed without tickets.

We arrived and took a look around: their side seemed almost like ours, only it didn't slope gradually and had a drop-off, like a step. I sat on the grass, on the edge of that step, and lowered my feet but couldn't reach the water. So I jumped, and immediately submerged, going blind and deaf. Then I opened my eyes and continued to sink, noticing little bubbles, like in boiling water, and tall, swaying blades of grass, like feathers. I touched the bottom, pushed off lightly, and went back up. The surface was very close—I could see the daylight; I stretched out my neck to gulp some air but immediately sank to the bottom again, with terrifying ease.

I could see myself from above as a curled little form descending facedown. If I'd known the word I'd have told myself that I resembled an embryo. Again I pushed off and rose to the surface, but this time I didn't dare lift my head and continued to bob on the water, staring helplessly into the slightly muddy darkness. I understood by then that I shouldn't try to lift my head. I was very light and floated easily but only if I didn't try to breathe. I was craving air, my ears filled with the deafening noise of running water. And then out of the corner of my eye I glimpsed an object dangling right next to me, like a willow branch. I extended my arms, grabbed it, and popped out of the water like a cork.

It turned out that a young woman had come to the riverbank to get water, leaned over to fill her buckets, saw something struggling underwater, thought it was a puppy, and wanted to hook it up with the shoulder yoke. Suddenly a child's hand shot out and grabbed it. The woman actually stepped back in fear, but too late: her catch stuck to the yoke like glue.

As for my friend, as soon as she saw that I wasn't coming up, she fled, like all children do when scared.

Shaking with cold, I tried to dry off in an abandoned kiosk in the company of my reappeared friend. Local brats were circling us, sniggering—look, a gal without clothes. My wet sundress clung to my skin. I was only seven or eight, but I knew it was suggestive of something improper and dirty. I tried to hide behind my friend. Playground laws are worse than sharia.

Samara's first public park, Strukovsky Garden.

It wasn't just my wetness. Like all severely malnourished children, I sported matchstick limbs and a swollen belly. Some brat pointed at me once in the street: "Look, a gal knocked up!" I believed him immediately. I didn't know how that happened, how long it took, or how it ended, but I did know that it was a secret and a disgrace, and so I only prayed, God, dear God, save me, save me. I had overheard this bit once; I didn't know any real prayers.

This imaginary pregnancy was the nightmare of my childhood. Who's hiding inside me? Is it a snake? A baby? Sometimes it growled, sometimes squeaked, sometimes bubbled. Oh, horror.

My friend and I got on the ferry; it was growing dark. Before going home I walked around the park clucking my teeth, trying to get a little drier—at home they forbade us categorically to go in the water . . .

The Durov
Theatre

W e spent our summers in that park near the water. Called
Strukovsky Garden, it was huge and overgrown, like a
forest, and descended all the way to the Volga. There we looked for
little round growths, like baby ferns, considered edible, and for
anything else we could put in our bellies. Sometimes it was our
only meal all day. Berries didn't grow in that park.

On Saturdays and Sundays music played in the park's band
shell.

When the Durov Animal Theatre was visiting Kuibyshev,
they set up a tent in Strukovsky; our job was to get inside without
tickets. The trick was to crawl into the tent on hands and knees,
together with the crowd—people stumbled on our backs but didn't
look down, wanting only to get in. It was important not to lose
balance, or else you could be crushed. Once inside, I needed to
sidle up to some couple and strike up a conversation, so the ushers
would think we were one family and I was their shaggy daughter.

That's how I got to see Durov's famous act with the elephant.
In the arena, they had erected an enormous bed with a gigantic

Vladimir Durov performing with an elephant in 1941.

pillow. The elephant sat on the bed and wound up the huge alarm clock, and it rang! Then the elephant lay down on its side, to the music of a lullaby. With some prodding from Durov, the elephant slowly stood up, lifted the pillow, and revealed a bedbug the size of a kettle. The elephant dropped the bedbug on the floor and stomped on it with an enormous foot. The bedbug exploded, to thunderous applause. Durov reached up and placed a treat in the elephant's mouth—it was like placing something on a top shelf.

Then there were monkeys. One, dressed in a black suit, leafed furiously through a thick volume, moving its fingers chaotically and greedily—there were treats hidden in its pages. The monkey shoved them into its mouth, glancing nervously over its shoulder, blinking and scratching. Its frenzied chewing and scratching resembled the motions of a hungry, lice-ridden boy.

Or girl.

Searching
for Food

Like stray puppies, we rooted around everywhere, looking for something to eat. One time I climbed into the cabin of an idling truck, looked into the compartment over the mirror, and saw three rubles! I showed them to the rest of the gang: "In here, inside the cabin!"

They all climbed in but found nothing. I felt triumphant. Naturally that money was taken from me, by the usual methods.

"Show us what you got!"

"I won't!"

"How about a kiss from my fist?"

"Just leave me alone, you morons."

"Let's go, guys. She got nothing, the whore's daughter."

"Hell I don't. Here, look!"

I opened my hand; someone slapped it from below; the money fell out and disappeared.

Late in the fall I returned to winter headquarters—that is, indoors, to my aunt and grandmother. One can't run barefoot in the snow. We had no winter boots, no clothes of any kind. No food either.

So I didn't attend school. But in September I stood on our balcony and watched the children walk to school, swinging their satchels. Along Frunze Street, a girl walked every morning dressed in a bright blue coat with large white buttons. How well I remember it! (When my son Kirill turned two, I managed to buy him and his little cousin Serezha blue flannel coats with white buttons. At that time it was extremely difficult to get anything at the store, and these were very simple flannel garments, but I was so happy to find them!)

Aunt Vava took home potato peels from the compost heap outside the Officers' Club. Granny baked them on a Primus stove without oil. I can still recall the stench of burning peel.

The Primus stove stood on the windowsill in our room. The neighbors had banished us from the shared kitchen.

We also looked for food in our neighbors' garbage. They were people of means. In Dedya's former room now lived an army major who owned a gramophone with a single record. Pressing my ear against the boarded-up door between our rooms, I memorized Beethoven's "Scottish Drinking Song" (*Come fill, fill, my good fellow!*) and an aria from the operetta *Silva* (*Beautiful dancers of a lovely cabaret, you were created for pleasure alone*). Our other neighbor was Rahil, the principal at the school for the railroad workers' children. My grandmother gave her a beautiful nickname—Fury. Fury had two daughters, older than me, and an equally scary husband, also a railroad boss.

The shared bathroom was heated with firewood, which we couldn't afford. Next to the wood stood an ax. We weren't allowed to use the bathroom, so we bathed with cold water in our room. One night we heard screams in the hallway. My poor old grandmother lay in a pool of blood outside the bathroom door. Fury's husband, on finding my grandmother in the bathroom, struck her on the head with the ax to teach her a lesson. Vava summoned an ambulance; the medics wrapped Granny's head in gauze—the only time anything white touched her skin in the fifteen years she lived in Kuibyshev. Naturally no one filed charges. The husband's nickname was Cretin. The whole family was called simply "crooks."

The army major, Cretin, and Fury left thick potato peels in their garbage, along with herring bones and sometimes cabbage leaves. Never any bread crusts. But to obtain even these riches, we somehow had to avoid insults and humiliation, so we foraged while the neighbors slept. If we had a little kerosene for the Primus stove, Granny made soup.

Dolls

One night, the usual moment came when the house quieted down. Hunger had completely devoured our insides, and after waiting the requisite period of time, the adults sent me to retrieve the neighbors' trash can. Remembering the ax, I tiptoed into the kitchen.

On a stool by the trash can reclined two large dolls, stripped of their clothes. They must have been discarded by Fury's daughters. Their noses were chipped, and they didn't have any hair; their soiled limbs and torsos were stuffed with rags.

I had a doll, but it was small, made of celluloid, and missing a leg. In addition, I owned a toy horse, which I had made from cardboard and painted with my only crayon, purple—I gave it an eye. The horse didn't seem very real, so I tried to flesh it out by wrapping a rag around its middle.

And here were two such incredible beauties!

Now, I know what a doll means to a girl: It is her tame goddess. It inspires worshipful adoration, furious possessiveness, and also a certain ferocity—it is mine, I can do what I want with it. Dolls are clutched to the breast and force-fed—and then abandoned without a glance. One can paint a doll's face, then scrub it off along with the factory paint. Shave its head. Perform surgeries on it. (One must take care to keep it away from boys—they will tear it apart.) Dolls are pitied and adored beyond words. Nothing surpasses a girl's passion for her doll—only her love for Mama, Papa, and grandparents.

I froze. I was staring at the discarded dolls, not believing my happiness. I knew we had no future together, that we'd have to part. I knelt before them, sat them up, and folded their poor soiled hands in their laps. Then I leaned my head against their soft torsos. They gradually filled my heart and my soul, as a child fills its mother's whole body when they embrace. They were so beautiful, so tall, so obedient.

I'm not sure how long this continued, maybe until dawn. Before leaving for work, Rahil stopped by the kitchen to check on her trash. Soon her girls sailed in, collected their dolls vengefully, and left.

Victory Night

And now the happiness, the Victory Night, for it was definitely night, not day, though no one slept.

Every hour that the announcement was expected, people kept repeating the magic formula: "Unconditional surrender." I was woken up by the noise outside, as though an enormous crowd were pushing through the street like a train. It was still dark, and we didn't have a clock, but I think it was around four, because the sun came up at five.

I ran outside as I was, in my sundress and barefoot, and spent the day running around the city.

Soldiers were being bounced everywhere, even the lazybones from our Officers' Club and, gently, the wounded from the military hospitals; on every corner gramophones, accordions, and balalaikas were playing; in Strukovsky Garden, a dance was organized; women were selling bunches of snowdrops at the gate.

A new life was beginning, and with it the great hunger of the postwar years.

Victory celebration in Moscow.

The Officers' Club

I spent more and more time on the streets.

The first time I ran away I must have been seven, soon after the victory.

In early June I spent several days in the wild. I didn't sleep in Strukovsky Garden: around there, all the usable spots had been defiled; through the cracks in the band shell I could see feces and mold. But I did find a spot—in the director's office at the Officers' Club.

Along with other kids, I had learned long since to get in past the guards of the Officers' Club to watch movies and learned to collect bread crumbs from the club's bread wagon after the driver and the cook took the last crate to the kitchen and the horse was resting with one hoof on tiptoe—that was when we, hungry children, climbed inside the wagon, where the smell of bread was indescribable, and scooped up crumbs off the floor.

The club's inner yard and main building were surrounded by sheds and garages. Guards chased away pigeons by throwing them bread crusts that landed on the tin roof of the shed and got stuck there, so the pigeons couldn't swallow them. Children from the nearby courtyards climbed onto that burning hot roof to look for dried crusts.

The only way to get to the roof was by standing on tiptoes on the edge of a huge barrel of tar. I don't know who left that barrel there—it was a perfect trap for hungry children. The bread crusts! For me, hunger was stronger than danger, and I always waited for the moment when the boys were not circling the barrel.

In the summer, the tar melted, seeped through the cracks, and formed an ugly black puddle around the barrel. Naturally I landed in it—somebody had pushed me.

I sat in the disgusting mess, trying not to cry. On all sides brats were squealing with laughter. I couldn't get up and only waved my hands slowly, watching them turn into black glass. A passerby finally unglued me, swearing the whole time. Accompanied by wild laughter I dragged myself home, trying not to touch my hair. At home, my poor relatives scrubbed me off the best they could, in the absence of soap or hot water. But my panties were ruined, and it was my only pair. I learned to tie my camisole between my legs.

All in all, by the standards of the time I had a relatively normal childhood. Courtyard friendships; hide-and-seek; cops-and-robbers. When we weren't running around wildly, we buried "treasures," placing shards of colored glass into a hole in the ground, covering them with a piece of clear glass, and then piling some dirty courtyard sand on top. We hunted for other kids' "treasures," guarding our own. In the courtyard I was mocked for my Moscow expressions, all those "the fact is" and "as you can see."

My closest and dearest companion was a dog, Damka. We would roll around, I would hug her skinny neck, we would jump and chase each other, or I would throw her a stick. But one day she ran away from me at a fantastic speed, dragging what looked like a bloodied hair comb: the kitchen workers at the club must have thrown away a rack of ribs. I ran after her, but for the first time she snarled at me. The time for jokes was over; Damka took food seriously, like the rest of us.

I tried to convince my aunt and grandmother to "give birth to at least a puppy, or at the very least a kitten."

One winter my dream came true, and I brought home a famished cat. It was New Year's Eve. The cat was sitting on the landing, waiting, meowing, and I let her in. Our kerosene lamp was burning on that special occasion, and the light was indescribably festive and beautiful. I was hugging my little Mura, who was meowing timidly. We waited till midnight to fetch the neighbors' trash, then celebrated with what they had discarded. The cat ate everything, it turned out, even herring heads and potato peels. After the meal, Mura and I walked in a circle around our Christmas tree: a fir branch stuck into a tin can. The cat walked clumsily on her skinny hind legs, and I held her by her front paws and belted out, "Beautiful dancers of a lovely cabaret," in harmony with the army major's gramophone. We had a holiday!

Then she meowed to be let out and ran off, never to return.

·   ·   ·

My whole life took place in the summer. Several times I actually managed to climb onto that cursed roof and find a bread crust. I couldn't jump down because of the barrel, so I dashed through the club's courtyard, past the guards. For us, the club offered an irresistible draw: in the evenings they showed trophy American movies with Errol Flynn and Deanna Durbin.

We watched every movie, hiding between showings behind the doors and especially in the drapes. One night I hid after the last show and stayed until everyone left. Then I flew down the empty hallways, as though in a dream, looking for a place to sleep, and found one: the director's office, where the felt couch scratched my cheek all night. I was about to fall asleep, but the night was very bright—it was June, and suddenly my sleepy eyes fell on the picture on the opposite wall: Marshal Voroshilov and Stalin appraising the troops in Red Square. For the first time I was terrified by a work of art.

Marshal Voroshilov and Joseph Stalin (second and third from the right) presiding over the May Day parade in 1926.

The Courtiers' Language

During the day, like many unsupervised children, I begged in the streets. I tolerated hunger reasonably well; we'd been starving for a long time. Granny lay in bed swollen like a mountain, although according to my aunt she did go occasionally to the port to help unload cargo ships, for which she received a bottle of raw spirits that could be exchanged for bread. Aunt Vava once brought home a handful of beet salad; another time it was plum jam, which I licked off her palm all at once like a little animal, understanding that it was my one and only chance to try it. For decades the smell of plums made me ill.

Our power had been shut off, but from time to time we managed to buy kerosene for the lamp and Primus stove. At the store we were helped after everyone else, for some reason, and had to wait for hours. Since then, I have associated the smell of kerosene with light and happiness. We could cook something on our stove. We could light the lamp, and the solemn, golden light flooded our room from the back of the couch.

I could tolerate hunger, but I couldn't tolerate lack of freedom. Fearing for me—a little girl from an educated family out and about in a city full of riffraff, not to mention a completely wild courtyard—my aunt and grandmother explained that gypsies had stolen a child, and under this pretext they forbade me to go out. I immediately disappeared, returning days later with an innocent explanation: I had been stolen by gypsies, and recovered by the police.

Aunt and Granny exchanged worried remarks over my head, using the so-called courtiers' language, the secret code of the underground revolutionaries. They didn't know that I had long since deciphered it. In that code, consonants were divided into two groups, and letters from the first group were substituted for letters from the second group; same with the vowels. So I could understand all their worries and fears, their plans and intentions, their bitter laments. But I didn't care, didn't believe them, and ignored their fears; my goal was to escape.

And that is how I spent the warm months of the war—flying about the city, begging, posing as an orphan: "No mommy, no daddy, please help."

The Bolshoi Theatre

One evening I was circling the Opera House. Inside, the lights were shining. A festive crowd was flowing in, and I could hear beautiful music. Plus it was warm inside. I couldn't get in through the main entrance, but I noticed a steep metal ladder that hugged the opera's wall—it must have been used by the light technicians and other staff.

Outside, it was drizzling and getting dark, with black clouds filling the sky. I started climbing the slippery ladder, barefoot, trying not to look down. Reaching the top, at least five floors above the ground, I rapped on the metal door: "No mommy, no daddy, please, Comrade, take pity on an orphan! I'm so cold, just five little minutes, just to listen to the music, please, dear Comrade . . ." The dark abyss and freezing wind must have added a note of genuine despair to my stock number: the door opened up and the kindly lighting technician allowed me into the warm darkness, flooded with the sounds of the orchestra.

I found myself on a little balcony next to the hot, smelly

View of the Opera House in Kuibyshev.

lights. Right below me, so close I could touch it, something magical, bright, and colorful was taking place—there was a palace among fake lilac bushes, with a balcony directly underneath mine, and on that balcony a beautiful pink lady was singing in a gentle voice, "My dear friend, I'm listening . . ." That night I listened to Rossini's *Barber of Seville*, performed by the evacuated Bolshoi Theatre. The next night I climbed the ladder again and rapped on the metal door, howling and frozen in my sundress, but wasn't let in.

I crawled back home like a punished dog. At least it was warm there. My whole life I remembered that duet between Rosina and Count Almaviva.

Later, when I came home from my wanderings, Granny and

Aunt no longer interrogated me, and pretended to believe my tales about gypsies. They were probably relieved that I was alive and didn't want to scare me away for good with questioning. Some nights they fed me cabbage soup, made from crushed leaves that Vava picked off the ground at the marketplace at the end of the day. "That's for your goat, right?" the seller women asked her, probably trying not to get upset. My aunt, a recent student of the military academy, burst into tears over those dirty, crushed cabbage leaves. Late at night, as usual, I was sent to the kitchen to retrieve our neighbors' garbage.

Down the Ladder

One day I must have spun such wild tales that after a whispered conversation in their secret language, Aunt and Granny came to a decision and immediately enforced it, locking the door from the inside and leaving the key in the keyhole.

They did it for a good reason. At a certain age every girl had to take her place in the courtyard's hierarchy. This usually involved being passed around behind the sheds. The older girls didn't discuss the process openly, only exchanged hints, pointing with their chins in that fearful direction.

I understood nothing. I didn't sense the danger, not yet. As thin as a skeleton, I was pummeled regularly but not yet used in that way. With time the older kids would have subjected me to the same fate, even if only to teach me a lesson, so that I would learn my place.

Suddenly denied freedom, I danced and sang across the room over to the door, ostensibly to demonstrate my prowess to my bedridden grandmother, and tried to grab the key—but was stopped by a pair of loving hands.

I thought for a bit, then stepped out on the balcony and looked down. We lived on the third floor—I couldn't jump. Terribly scared, I reached for the next balcony and then for the fire escape—a rickety worm-eaten ladder with missing rungs. Hanging by my fingertips, I felt my way down to the last rung. Five feet above the ground, the ladder ended. I flopped on my backside, then sprang back up. I was free! It was a bright, sunny day. I was prepared: I had my entire wardrobe on—camisole, sundress, plus a cotton vest, given to me by a kindly neighbor who also occasionally fed me bread.

Trembling with happiness, I strolled under our balcony, until I saw my aunt's completely gray head (she was thirty-two). I stared into her huge, dark blue eyes. "How did you get down?" she shouted, trying to gain some time, hoping that Granny would somehow crawl down the stairs on her swollen legs and catch me. "Jumped off the balcony!" I lied, just in case, and skipped off.

For good, as it turned out. I saw them again nine years later: I was eighteen, and they didn't recognize me. "Who is it?" my tiny grandmother whispered.

The terrible guilt I felt.

Literary Sleep-Ins

In the winters before my escape, my grandmother was educating me and keeping me from running away using her special talent: she could recount from memory the Russian classics, word for word.

A graduate of the elite Bestuzhev Institute for Young Ladies, my grandmother possessed a fantastic memory. Her former husband, my grandfather Nikolai Yakovlev, was a famous professor of linguistics who knew eleven languages. But I, their offspring, didn't even attend grade school, for lack of shoes. From April to October I ran barefoot, and winters I stayed indoors. Still, I learned how to read—from the newspapers that our neighbors left in the trash. I could recite from memory excerpts from my grandmother's favorite bedside tome, *History of the Communist Party of the Soviet Union: Short Course*, in which she had underlined the most obnoxious lies. The whole book was covered in red pencil.

There were two other books in the house: *A Room in the*

Attic by Vanda Vasilevskaya, which left no impression, and a biography of Cervantes by Bruno Frank. In that book, there was a description of a crystal decanter with red wine standing on a table in what I remember was a prison cell. Red shadows fell on the white cloth. Nothing like that existed in my world. There was no red and no white. But still it was present in my childhood life—that's what matters. I remember those shadows! And that tablecloth, white and thick like old snow, with heavy folds along the corners. I could see that scene as though I lived in it. The room with thick wooden beams. Small, low windows aglow from the setting sun. Green fields outside. That's how I imagined, for some reason, a Spanish prison.

My grandmother also owned a volume of Mayakovsky's poems—probably in memory of his courtship, of his youthful love for her, when he called her baroquely the Blue Duchess, in the spirit of reigning poetic style. Roman Jakobson had brought Mayakovsky to the Moscow Linguistic Circle, introducing him as a genius he had discovered. There Mayakovsky met with my grandmother for the second time. Before that he had courted her when they were both teenage members of the Party. At the circle, according to family legend, Mayakovsky proposed, and my grandmother refused him. And by 1914 she and Nikolai Yakovlev already had a daughter, my aunt Vava.

When Granny returned to Moscow in 1956, after her rehabilitation, her sister Asya, who had also returned from the labor camp and exile, asked her: "So, you refused to marry a poet and married a professor instead. How did *that* work out?"

Our literary sleep-ins took place in the wintertime.

Our usual position was in bed, Granny towering over my

bone-thin body like a mountain—so swollen from hunger was she. We covered ourselves with every rag we owned, and for days on end she recited classics from memory, primarily Gogol—*Dead Souls*, *Evenings on a Farm near Dikanka*. She had one weakness: she lavished too much attention on the descriptions of meals and innocently inserted mysterious items like borscht and bacon. When she explained what they were, I salivated like Pavlov's dog.

She also read Gogol's "The Portrait" and *Viy*, which scares me to this day. "The Portrait," a story of a young artist compelled by a mysterious portrait to sell his talent, left me dazzled. To this day I considered its subject, bartering one's gift for the worldly glory, the most important among humanity's collective tales.

My Performances.

Green Sweater

In the summertime I begged. I didn't beg by holding out a hand on street corners, no. I performed, like Édith Piaf.

Usually I looked for a quiet spot near the sheds, where children and grandmas liked to congregate, and then began my program. They were cheesy, lowbrow numbers beloved by washerwomen and lumpen proletarians: "In a Clearing near School"; "Along the Dewy Track"; "On Berlin's Cobblestones." Tango tunes I skipped; the most popular tango of the time, "The Tired Sun," I hated with a passion. Every night they played that record in Strukovsky Garden; to its sound, the wounded shuffled over to dance, the village women peddled flowers at the gate, the endless sunsets finished burning, the tired sun indeed set behind the Volga, and later we would step over flower heads stuck on a wire. For a long time I racked my brain— why the wire? That's how they kept broken daisies together.

(I was so fed up with "The Tired Sun" that I wrote it into the script for an animated film by Yuri Norstein, *The Fable of Fables*, about our shared postwar childhood. That film is broadcast every year on Victory Day.)

Then, like a parrot, I rattled off the record that our neighbor, the army major, played every night in his room. First the "Scottish Drinking Song"—"Come fill, fill, my good fellow!"—followed by the finale, the potpourri from the musical *Silva*.

Beautiful dancers of a lovely cabaret,
You were created for pleasure alone.
To you the doubts of love are unknown.

I usually stumbled on "unknown," but still.

If my repertory ran out but the circle of children and grandmas seemed numerous enough, I quickly switched gears to recite Gogol's "The Portrait." The children were stunned. One time, someone gave me a slice of black bread. Another, a shy little boy approached and said his mama wanted to see me. Instinct warned against visiting strange apartments, but the other children were curious, too, and talked me into going. We all walked up the dark stairs, a door opened, and a woman with a face wet with tears offered me a green open cardigan that I put on immediately. Everyone rejoiced at my acquisition and looked me over with pride, as if I were their successful creation.

I never "toured" that courtyard again. We avoid places where we've endured pain, but the opposite is true, too. Extreme kindness can be repaid only with ingratitude. What if the miracle won't repeat itself and life's greatest consolation—remembering the kindness shown to us—disappears? Those little faces won't be there, and the green sweater won't be offered. This way, they are always with me. The crowd of hungry children, the dark stairs, the open door, the outstretched hand, and someone's mother, crying, her face invisible against the light.

The Portrait

And so, after a day of reciting Gogol's "The Portrait" in the courtyards, I found myself in the director's room at the Officers' Club, on the scratchy couch, and, resting my head on my arm for a pillow, saw in the light of an endless sunset that particular portrait, in which Stalin seemed ready to turn around and fix me with his beady black eyes. Terrified, I quickly turned to my other side and covered my eyes.

The figure in the painting exuded malice. After that, I always slept in other offices. Who knows what the artist must have felt when he was working on it? He may have been fearing for his life, hoping for mercy.

After receiving the green sweater, I developed a strange shyness and couldn't perform anymore. I had to move my begging act indoors, into a store. My artistic career stalled until I found myself in a children's home.

The Story of
a Little Sailor

But begging in a store is much harder! You tap someone on the shoulder. "Please, Comrade, give us a kopeck." And they give you a kopeck, but the smallest ice cream costs three rubles. You mumble and edit your request, and they reasonably object that this is what you asked for. The formula "spare a kopeck" must have survived from before the revolution, when a kopeck was actually worth something.

My debut took place in a large grocery store. Beggars formed an honor guard next to the cash register. Customers passed through our double ranks on their way to pay, then turned around to face a human wall of misery.

As I remember it, that store was almost empty of customers; its high shelves were empty of goods, too. In those days, goods were delivered unpredictably and then "tossed out" onto the shelves: the customers rushed inside, quickly formed a line, and in the end "obtained" something or other.

I took my place at the end of the long line of beggars. There was zero hope.

Suddenly the situation changed. The honor guard had annoyed the cashier long enough; she yelled at them from her little window, and they meekly crawled over to the back wall. But I stayed. Right below the cash register was a little ledge, to catch the change, and I squeezed myself under it, away from the angry cashier's eyes. I was too tall and had to bend my neck painfully.

My God, people stampeded to shower me with change—the pocket of my sundress under the green sweater ballooned. I felt a little scared, not understanding: Why were they giving me all this money?

Then I understood: my crooked neck looked like an exotic injury. My face, I suppose, expressed genuine suffering: to remain in one position, with a crooked neck, is unbearable for a child. But I endured—after getting lucky with my little nook, I couldn't just abandon it. I must have looked like a little martyr. Other beggars were seen there every day and lost their appeal. Now here was something different, a new sample of misery, a crippled little girl.

The last straw was a boy beggar, who solemnly gave me his penny, then returned meekly to his legless father by the far wall. When I realized what was happening, I felt a burning shame. My heart stopped. What disgrace awaited me if they found out I wasn't crippled! My face turned even redder. People approached me, asked me questions. Keeping my neck even more crooked, I unglued myself from my nook and shuffled past the beggars to the door. Outside, I continued my act a little longer. Finally, I snuck into a courtyard and counted my riches: fourteen rubles!

I could buy an ice cream. The smallest portion cost three rubles, the medium nine, the large twelve. But I nurtured a dream about a doll. It lived in my imagination, tall and beautiful. I flew over to the little stationery store that sold toys. I visited it often, just to stare at the toys, and was regularly expelled, but this time was different—I had money. In emotional agony, I scooped out my change and dumped it onto the counter. The seller counted the money sternly: my riches could buy me only the cheapest item in the store. Under the glass counter lay a little boy sailor with a celluloid head and stuffed limbs. The more expensive girl was beyond my means. My tears unspent, my hopes dashed, I accepted the toy sailor and stuffed it under the green sweater next to my heart.

But then I paused. Then I thought for a bit. Then I hugged the doll tightly. He was mine. My own little baby. I took off

Panorama of postwar Kuibyshev.

down the street, jumping with happiness. I had my own little boy!

When I ran into our courtyard, the little sailor wasn't under my sweater. I had dropped it running. My luck ran out. I knew it was justice. I had deceived everyone, and God had punished me. My little sailor had warmed my breast for a very short time.

My New Life

Soon after this tragedy a miracle occurred. After my escape down the ladder I lived on the street—that is, in the courtyard—for several days, performing during the day and spending nights at the Officers' Club. I was even adopted by a woman who had lost her child; she lived in a little house nearby, under a huge shade tree. The child's bed stood under a portrait crossed with a black ribbon. The woman bathed me in a tub and anointed my hair with kerosene, for lice. The woman was dark and small. She avoided looking at me directly and kept going through her daughter's precious clothes, not ready to part with them yet, wanting first to get used to me. I slept under the portrait one night, then escaped back into our courtyard. For some reason I was still waiting for my own mother. She had left four years before and was sending us money transfers with which we bought kerosene and black bread.

Free as a bird, shaggy, covered with lice and bedbug bites, probably all dusty again after the bath (there was no mirror; like all tramps, I didn't know what I looked like), I was flying around our courtyard. Suddenly I spotted my enemies: a brother and sister, both older than me, from the apartment upstairs, who always hit me and shooed me away. I hid in a corner, but they smiled nicely and said I must come with them, that my mommy was waiting for me upstairs. My mommy? Which mommy? That dark woman with the funereal portrait? And why should I go to my enemies' house? But the brats kept shouting, "Your mommy came for you from Moscow."

Incredible. I felt dizzy.

Street children don't trust anyone. What if they were trying to lure me back home, under lock? Or get me sent to an orphanage? Two ladies from the welfare department were looking for me, I knew. Once, I tapped on someone's back. "Please, Comrade, spare a kopeck." The back turned, and there she was—the welfare dragon. How I ran!

I followed my enemies. We walked past the door to the apartment, where my poor aunt and grandmother were waiting in vain for me, walked up another floor, and there, at the kitchen table, sat my own mother.

I couldn't breathe. I hadn't seen my only one for four years. Her face was smiling, but I could see the dimples under her eyes that always appeared when she was about to cry (my daughter has them, too). She sat me down and began to spoon-feed me hot cereal she had made while waiting for me, with milk, butter, and sugar. I threw up. My mother cleaned me and carried me over to the public baths, like the five-year-old I used to be. There the bath workers shaved my head, leaving only a tiny fringe. That night we spent at the airport, in a huge room filled with sleeping people. We slept on canvas cots under clean white sheets that smelled of sun and summer; my mother held my hand. I couldn't sleep. Clean sheets and my mother's closeness kept me awake.

The date was June 9, 1947. I remember it always. We were woken up and put on a plane with long metal benches. We flew for a long time, bouncing through turbulence. We arrived in the morning. I was dressed in new brown sandals, underwear, a camisole, a bright red dress, a new plaid coat. I felt like Cinderella at the ball, completely out of my element. A new life was beginning. There was no room in it for me.

The Metropol Hotel

Moscow that day was chilly and cloudy. A light fog obscured Sverdlov Square. The sun wasn't out yet. I was tired and cold; my mother never stopped holding my hand.

We crossed the empty Okhotny Market and walked over to the Metropol Hotel, where my great-grandfather Ilya—Dedya—was waiting for us. I was amazed there were so few cars at the intersection: I grew up watching American trophy movies and expected to find myself in New York, with its rivers of cars. But we arrived in postwar Moscow.

In the Metropol, Dedya occupied a private room. That's where I was brought from the maternity ward, where I spent the first years of my life. It was my home, sort of.

But by that point, after the war, after the separation, I had become an unmanageable, wild child, a real Mowgli. Today they would have called me asocial. In Kuibyshev we led the life of pariahs, untouchables. "Enemies of the people" wasn't an empty phrase. We were enemies to everyone: to our neighbors, to the

View of Moscow's main thoroughfare after the war.

police, to the janitors, to the passersby, to every resident of our courtyard of any age. We were not allowed to use the shared bathroom, to wash our clothes, and we didn't have soap anyway. At the age of nine I was unfamiliar with shoes, with handkerchiefs, with combs; I didn't know what school or discipline was. I couldn't sit still; I read books at a fantastic speed crouching on the floor. I swallowed food instantly, using my hands primarily, and licked the plates clean. Bedbugs and lice bit my arms to bloody scabs; my hands and feet were gray and cracked, the cracks filled with pus. My nails were black, like a monkey's. Only my eyes and hair must have remained the same. But my hair had been shaved.

This is what my mother received after four years.

Naturally I didn't fit with the Metropol establishment. In the morning my mother left for work. Dedya also went out on business. I was left alone. I got bored. I rummaged through Dedya's desk and came across a jar of silver half-rubles. Below, in the courtyard, brats were running around, screaming. From the windowsill I began to throw silver coins at them; each coin caused a new explosion of howling and fighting.

The next day I donned Dedya's peaked cavalry cap, which reached down to my chin, lifted his saber off the wall, saddled the toy wooden horse I found in the room (it had belonged to my young great-uncle Serezha, who was a pilot), and proceeded to gallop down the gleaming hallways, screaming, "Hurray, comrades, attack!" Imagine an enormous cavalry cap on top of a wooden horse and a huge saber bouncing off the beautiful floor. I was very small and thin; later, in the children's home, I was called Matchstick Muscovite.

Mumsy

Angry words must have been exchanged, and I was promptly removed from the Metropol. Dedya's wife and other relatives asked us out. At first my mother took me to the house of our almost relative, a tiny old woman with a crooked back who lived in the summerhouse area called Silver Forest. Everyone called her Mumsy; she was a person of enormous kindness. She had raised the husband of Dedya's youngest daughter, Lena; both were shot in 1937. She earned her living making women's clothes. Her most popular creations were brassieres: a client of hers had brought one from France; Mumsy copied it and began supplying the neighborhood with homemade lingerie.

Even though we were not related, Mumsy took me in without a word. The house was full of people, including her grandchildren and great-grandchildren. But I didn't have time for introductions: I wanted to hear what my mother was telling Mumsy, but they went inside. After making secret arrangements, my mother kissed me—her dimples appeared—and left.

I had carefully memorized the route from the bus stop to the house and a little later escaped out the gate and found my way back. My plan was to reach a subway station and ask how to find the "Lazar Kaganovich station." But I was wrong. I remember a small crowd of sympathetic people who were trying to convince me that the entire subway system was named after Lazar Kaganovich. They even walked me over to the Sokol station and showed me the inscription on the entrance: "The Sokol Station of the Moscow Subway System Named in Honor of Lazar Kaganovich."

I felt as if I were in the fairy tale about Aladdin, where all doors were marked with the same sign. Damn that Kaganovich, I thought. People were talking about calling the police and welfare services. Luckily, I fished out a name, "Metropol Hotel." People laughed with relief and led me to the subway, and someone even convinced the guard to let me in for free. I must have told the credulous Muscovites God knows what about myself—that I was an orphan and hadn't eaten for six days. A little later I showed up, victorious, at the Metropol, like Tom Thumb, who couldn't get lost. Mama gasped upon hearing that I was at Dedya's again. Dedya's wife must have gasped, too. I was removed from Dedya's and promptly packed off to a summer camp.

Summer Camp

There was no running away from there. First, we traveled by boat; then, against the setting sun, we traversed an immense meadow through the ringing of mosquitoes and the aroma of wet grass. We were dragging suitcases and satchels; many of the kids were older than me, bigger and stronger. It was useless to memorize the route. For the first time I found myself in a place I couldn't escape from.

The rules of the wild courtyard where I grew up were simple: run, grab, swallow, hide; meet a punch with a punch; if someone calls you, don't go. Camp regulations couldn't be more different. Here, some of the amazing facts were: four daily meals; clean sheets; a personal towel; a common bath once a week; a real latrine, instead of squatting in a corner; a trough for washing feet before bedtime; and marching in a column everywhere: to the cafeteria four times a day; to the bedroom twice; to the parade ground twice on regular days and once extra on holidays; also, to the woods.

Very quickly it was discovered that I didn't belong to the Young Pioneers, so I was inducted, very solemnly, and given a red tie. Soon, equally solemnly, to the sound of drums, I was expelled. I don't remember what for, exactly; probably for constant scuffles and completely uncivilized behavior. They didn't even know that I had never attended school!

I lost all my things as soon as we arrived. The only clothes that survived was my parade uniform: a white blouse and a black skirt on suspenders. They must have been at the bottom of the suitcase. The button for one of the suspenders disappeared immediately. I tucked the suspender under my skirt, and it dragged behind me like a tail, often wet, because it rained a lot that summer. Naturally I was mocked.

Overwhelmed by these difficulties, I even made myself an idol to pray to: a little branch stuck in the soil in front of a pine tree, which I adorned with flowers that soon wilted. I prayed to my idol fervently, on my knees. In Kuibyshev, I had begun to believe in God; I just figured out one day that God exists. My faith expressed itself in crossing myself after yawning, as I saw an old woman do on a streetcar once.

My previous life had taught me to be extraordinarily sparing with food. Behind my bed I was saving petrified gingerbread that my mother had given me for the road. I was saving it for a rainy day and also as a sacred connection with Mama. One day, a sanitary commission was examining our dorm and discovered my hoard, to my terrible shame. The gingerbread was in a satchel made from my old flannel underpants, and that, too, seemed to shock the commission. Oh, how miserable I was there.

Camp nurtured in me a hatred of constant supervision and

Summer of 1949. Camp. One of the suspenders is still attached.

collectivism of any kind, and at the same time admiration to the point of tears at the sight of a marching squad; humility and suspicion of praise; a desire to make myself inconspicuous and simultaneously to participate in all talent-based activities—to draw, to dance, to recite from the stage, to act, to make theater costumes from nothing.

For the camp carnival I dressed up as a clown: a bushy wig (made with gauze and bits of hemp pulled out from the walls of a wooden barracks), a red nose painted with beet juice, and a ladle pinched from the kitchen to represent a clown's umbrella. I was strolling and prancing under my ladle, hoping to receive the first prize—an unlimited supply of cranberry juice. But no one even noticed me. So I decided to go and look for that juice on my own—it must have been somewhere!—and in the dark corner by the kitchen discovered a huge barrel. The ladle came in handy; I scooped up the red liquid and took a gulp, rejoicing that no one was chasing me away because I hadn't won the prize.

The liquid turned out to be filthy water in which they had washed beets and other vegetables for lunch. The disgusting taste of dirty beet tops. Another lesson of communal life: Do not attempt to look for free stuff by yourself. Also: Where there is no crowd, there's nothing worth having.

Camp also developed in me an exaggerated sense of fairness, a love of strikes and protests, a need to insist on my position, and a proclivity for small-time mischief, like stealing a cucumber from a state-owned patch. Children's honor code forbade self-promotion, hoarding, snitching, and stealing personal property (state property didn't count; no one stole anything else).

At the end of the summer I was returned to my mother with an empty suitcase, dressed in a skirt with two tails—all the buttons were gone.

Chekhov Street.
Grandpa Kolya

O ur next port of call was the home of my mother's father, Nikolai Yakovlev, my grandpa Kolya, at 29 Chekhov Street, Apartment 37. There, too, figured an evil stepmother with a daughter. A wizened hag of forty-five, the stepmother was our endless nightmare. Every month she dragged Mama to court, trying to kick us out.

Grandpa had a private room, but it was half the size of Dedya's, about 120 square feet, with fifteen-foot ceilings. The bookcases containing his library, five thousand volumes, reached all the way to the ceiling. There was a separate bookcase for the Bibles—the largest, of white pigskin with silver clasps, was too heavy to lift. There was an original edition of *Boris Godunov*. There was *Eugene Onegin*; the bookseller who bought it from us believed that it had once belonged to General Yermolov, one of the defeaters of Napoleon's army. The secret trip to the bookseller took place because that year I had had a series of sinus infections from which I couldn't recover, and Mama wanted to take me to the Baltic. In the entire library I could read only one book: *The Description of the Land of Kamchatka* by Stepan Krasheninnikov. It had the sour smell of old paper. The other 4,997 volumes were in foreign languages: for example, the complete works of Goethe illustrated with Gustave Doré's nightmarish figures with horns.

Grandpa was a professor of linguistics and knew eleven languages, plus seventy dialects of the Caucasus, for which he had created alphabets based on the Latin script to replace the old Arabic-based ones. For some remote villages he had to invent a written language. He is believed to have developed the theory of phonemes, in 1923, and the mathematical method in linguistics. Recently, the *Independent* newspaper referred to him as the Father of Alphabets. In the twenties he wanted to convert Cyrillic into the Latin script. He was an authority among Slavists, linguists, and mathematicians.

Grandpa Kolya was over six feet tall and wore size 12 shoes: both my feet could fit into one of his overshoes. He spoke very little. When his ex-wife wanted to instill another wicked idea in him, she tapped on his back and asked, "Kolya, may I come in?"

After he was fired and denounced, his favorite occupation became leafing through antique maps of Europe. He had been the deputy director of the Institute of Oriental Studies, an academic star. Now he didn't have a penny; pupils and colleagues had abandoned him. He spent his days in an armchair in the hallway, smoking shag, writing on scrolls of gray paper in a perfect calligraphic hand, and leafing through his favorite maps, showing tiny villages—in his mind, he was walking the old routes.

Grandpa was fired because he wasn't quick enough to praise Stalin's article "Marxism and Problems of Linguistics."

He couldn't sleep. At night, lying high on his metal-mesh bed, he would slap his knees, hard, and scream obscenities at his enemies. He could smoke two packs of shag a night, whispering and occasionally screaming his useless damnations. In our tiny room, one could slice the smoke with a knife. I learned to sleep with my head clutched between my elbows.

My grandfather had lost everything. He had been elected a corresponding member at the Academy of Sciences; he lived like any prominent, well-off professor, supporting his ex-wife and his youngest daughter, who was ill with Graves' disease, and also another family of his: a fat, red-haired woman named Fanya and her daughter, who lived in the same building. He would go to their home for Sunday lunch and then rest there. I tagged along, because of the food. After lunch, I tucked him in on the couch for a nap.

One Sunday, Fanya served cherry compote for dessert. I had never tasted anything so delicious and just kept on eating; in the end I consumed the whole jar. The same night I was taken to the hospital with acute appendicitis. They put me on a table, secured my hands and feet, and gave me a mask with ether. The gas was tearing at my lungs, and I fought and begged them to let me have one breath of air, just one, and they did, but then they finished the torture, and I went under.

I was flying through a wide tunnel. Its walls were punctured by thin, burning rays of white light that felt like a lashing rain. I flew through those poisonous white needles, my ears filled with an unpleasant swishing sound. I was flying toward a patch of brightest light—a full picture of clinical death, as described by survivors . . .

Trying to Fit In

Besides bookcases, Grandpa's room contained a full bed, a huge mahogany desk, an armchair, a tall filing cabinet, and a square dinner table.

My mother had slept under that table since 1943. It had one enormous drawback: five inches above the floor, its legs were connected with a thick plank, so that one had to sleep with her feet either over that plank or under it, which was extremely uncomfortable. That's why my mother arranged a bed for me in the common hallway, on top of Grandpa's trunk. I went to sleep there eagerly; I had never slept alone before. I spent two nights on the trunk, listening to the rustling of electric meters, one per room. Then, under the stepmother's leadership, other neighbors removed the trunk and replaced it with an enormous wardrobe. I returned to Mama's side, under the dinner table. It was our little home. On the table, we kept utensils and foodstuffs; underneath, around the mattress, our clothes were piled up.

But the stepmother couldn't leave us alone. Soon she had

another idea for how to improve our life. One day she showed up with movers: she had decided she needed the table for her summerhouse. Mama wept and tried to catch our falling things. A tough street kid, I grabbed one of the legs and wouldn't let go. Our universe was collapsing. Stepmother stood in the doorway, issuing commands in a military voice. The pleased neighbors strolled up and down the corridor, observing this scene. The table was removed. We sat among our things in an empty space, as though after a bombing.

My mother didn't break under this blow. She finished crying, took in the newly empty space with fresh eyes, measured it with a tape measure, and soon bought us a little desk and a bed— and they fit! The bed had a secret: one section folded, becoming a seat for the desk during the day, and at night it turned back into a bed. Now I could do my homework sitting up, like normal people. The bed wasn't very wide: thirty inches for the two of us, and I wasn't tiny anymore. In the evening, happy that I could lie down, I tossed and howled with joy; at night I kicked and turned and Mama complained about my sharp elbows. We slept together for seven more years, until I completely grew up, and then Mama bought me a folding cot, which, miraculously, also fit. My happiness couldn't be described. I had my own bed!

I will mention just one more episode with the evil stepmother. I was in my grandfather's bed with a high fever; the apartment was empty except for the stepmother. In my fever I thought the ceiling and the walls were collapsing in on me. I ran out of the terrible room and flew down the hallway, looking for any living soul, and came upon the stepmother. She heard me out, grabbed me by the shoulder with her bony hand, walked me back to the room, shoved me into the bed, and then locked the door from the outside. I screamed and threw myself at the door for hours. How long it lasted, who opened up for me, I don't remember.

My terror that day could be compared only to what I felt during the children's play I saw in Kuibyshev. I must have been quite small. The play featured King Bone, a Russian fairy-tale character. For a while he was hiding under the stage, but then the secret trapdoor lifted and he appeared in an unearthly green light, rising slowly to his full height: a skeletal old man, covered with moss and jangling chains. My desperate cries filled the theater. After that he came to me in my dreams several times. In one dream I saw myself walking on an empty street, at dawn, past a row of squat yellow houses, and in the window above one door I saw the familiar green light. The door was about to open; I sprinted down the sidewalk and caught up with a passerby. "Excuse me, sir," I asked him cleverly, "but shouldn't we end this terrible dream?" And then I woke up.

Later, in a film by Luis Buñuel, *The Discreet Charm of the Bourgeoisie*, I saw a similar scene—a soldier's dream. He was also walking past low-rise buildings, in a city of the dead, and one of the entrances was filled with crumbling soil. In one of my fairy tales, "The Black Coat," a girl runs through an empty street in a city where she alone is alive.

Children's Home

I had to be enrolled somewhere; at the very least, I needed to start school. So the moment came when my mother made some biscuits for the road and sent her daughter to Bashkiria, to a facility for sickly children, in the company of a woman traveling in the same direction.

We traveled for several days. I was offering my soggy biscuits to everyone on the train. From the station we walked for a long time. It was fall. I remember a golden forest with its smells of fallen leaves and smoke, and the fragrance of fresh water and algae coming from the river.

The school, a two-story former palace, stood on the high bank of the river Ufimka, outside the town of Ufa. (In those days, orphanages, boarding schools, and children's centers occupied former palaces. Monasteries were used as mental asylums, prisons, and juvenile colonies.)

On learning that I could read and write, the staff placed me in second grade. I was issued a notebook. For the first time I held

The river Ufimka in the fall.

a real pen. I dipped it into the inkwell and began to spell. The teacher came up to me. "Why are you writing in the middle of the page? You need to start from the top." I tore out the page and on the next one wrote "Class Work" and the date, again in the middle, like a dissertation title. Again the teacher told me to start at the top. Once more I started in the middle. The teacher's patience was exhausted; I was transferred to first grade.

There, I quickly became an academic star, which didn't stop me from behaving in the same manner as at the summer camp. Once more, I was expelled from the Young Pioneers.

When I fell ill with strep, I was sent to the infirmary, which was also called the "isolation ward." I was lying on a very clean white cot, dizzy with fever, locked in, completely alone, terribly scared. What joy it was to see a little white mouse sitting under the adjacent bed! I gave it the piece of bread I was saving under the pillow. She took it with her front paws, sat down on her tail like a squirrel, and started nibbling.

Later, we were preparing for the New Year's pageant. Our teachers were all Leningrad residents who were evacuated along with the children during the blockade. They gave us a full-scale theatrical show. I was dressed as a gypsy, in full skirts and a floral shawl, plus a necklace of Christmas-tree beads over my skinny chest. First we sang kneeling on the floor, swaying and waving, and then I danced solo, swirling my skirts.

I knew well the life of a gypsy camp from my time in Kuibyshev. Every summer, after the Volga stopped flooding, gypsies set up tents on our bank and made stew in pots over a fire. It was the stew that attracted us. Fires were burning; a bear with a ring in its nose was roaring on a chain; filthy kids were running everywhere, dressed in overalls with holes between the legs—a brat squatted, did his business through the hole, stood up, and kept on running. I can no longer remember how they danced, but at the children's home, during the concert, I danced just like they did.

That performance brought me my first suitor—a blond second-grader, the well-mannered son of a teacher. I treated him as a young lady should, and we never even had a scuffle.

I had no clothes to wear outside. I wrote to my mother, and a miracle happened: a large box arrived containing felt boots and a coat lined with faux fur, with an ink spot on the hem, the legacy of my second cousin. Ecstatic, I ran outside and swirled and ran around on the icy pond. The felt boots were magically warm and comfortable. I didn't notice how my foot fell through a little hole in the ice. I was sitting there, yelling, for some reason, "Hurray, Comrades," so no one noticed right away that I'd become one-legged. When they pulled me out, it was too late: the new boot had sunk all the way to the bottom.

By spring there were fewer children left, and in May everyone was gone. The facility for the weakened children was closing for summer vacation or even shutting down for good—recent years had been plagued with poor harvests and famine. The teachers left. My little suitor left, too. Manya, who was in the same classroom, also went home. She was fourteen but so weak she couldn't hold a pen, and was sent to the first grade. She was extremely thin and walked poorly; she had huge black eyes.

Our palace emptied and was shut down. Only the custodian remained, with her boyfriend; they lived in the groundskeeper's house, and I lived with them. They spoke Bashkirian; I still remember how to count in that language.

The couple gathered snowdrops in the woods, to sell at the market in town. I went along, to make myself useful. I had to find a place in that strange suspended life. We set out at first light. In huge forest meadows we looked for little white stars in the thick grass, so dark it seemed blue. We plucked unopened buds, whole baskets of them.

The custodian and her lover talked between themselves, and I could understand them, having lived eight months in Bashkiria. They were saying that my mother had abandoned me and that I would be sent to an orphanage as soon as there was an official decision about me. I didn't believe them. Later I learned that it was just another family trait—we are always late, for everything.

During the day I explored the local woods. There one could visit the famous Pugachev's Cave. The entrance was a narrow crack. Behind it, rumor held, lay huge underground chambers. I circled that crack for days, but something always stopped me— instinct told me to stay away from tight, narrow spaces. On one of my rambles I came across a cabin. An elegant lady was sitting by the window, smoking a cigarette. I asked for a smoke, and she gave me one. Very professionally I imitated a smoker—I didn't even cough. The lady watched me with interest. How did a beauty like her end up in the middle of the woods?

I told her my usual fibs about being an orphan and all alone in the world. She would have adopted me, I'm sure, had I stayed in the woods.

I Want to Live!

Finally someone came to take me home. I was ten by then, with a year of school behind me. It was a long journey. Along the way, my initial companion vanished and was replaced by others. For several days I stayed in someone's house, slept on the floor. The mother pitied me and expressed a wish to keep this incredible orphan who invented such outrageous stories.

But I didn't let her adopt me. I disliked her immediately, seeing her as someone who wanted to steal my mother's property. I belonged to my mother with every cell; I worshipped her; the memory of her face kept me warm, metaphorically speaking, in the life of a virtual orphan that I led, despite having a living father, grandmother, grandfather, aunt, and a whole pack of cousins. I had one objective in life: to live with my mother.

When I finally reached Moscow I was immediately shipped off again, to another summer camp, again for three months, for another painful attempt to socialize me.

At the children's home I was a recognized star and an A

student. Here I was immediately demoted: first from head of a squad, to which I was elected for my fantastic enthusiasm and perfect behavior in the first few days (I think); then, as usual, from the Young Pioneers. The reason wasn't hard to guess: constant scuffles, zero discipline, and so on. My handkerchiefs, sandals, ribbons, combs, and socks I didn't see after the first week. As punishment, I was soon transferred to the younger squad. There I immediately joined in a general scuffle, took a good beating, and continued in my usual wild manner.

My only consolation was in art. I signed up for the choir, the theater, the drawing class, and the dance class. With my talents I hoped to achieve recognition by the camp society—postwar children who grew up in conditions of total famine and old-school discipline. But I can't remember a single case in which a child was respected for her singing and drawing. At the camp, singers and actors were treated with contempt, as in the Middle Ages. The campers respected what is usually respected in an individual: a disdainful attitude, silence, composure, readiness for anything—in other words, strong character. Self-respect also counted, but first and foremost came primitive physical strength.

My reputation rested on one skill: after lights-out I told "scary" stories. I remember one night at my beloved children's home: I couldn't stop spinning my scary yarns, everyone was already asleep, and suddenly I fell into a panic—I realized for the first time that someday I would die. I was convulsing in my bed, screaming, "I don't want to die, I don't want to die, I want to live!" The lights went on, everybody was up, the grown-ups were holding me down, and I fought them and screamed terribly.

I had already seen death once, from our balcony in Kuibyshev. There was a truck parked right underneath; in the back, on sky-blue pillows, lay a dead girl, dressed like a doll. I had wept all night.

The next time I wept like that was in the fall of 1949, after my return from the camp. My mother told me that Dedya, my great-grandfather, had died a year earlier. Dedya died in 1948,

The last photograph of Ilya Veger, my great-grandfather, in November 1948. Children would address him as Father Frost.

eleven years after his children Lena, Asya, and Zhenya were sentenced to "ten years without the right to correspondence." Several times he walked over to Lubianka, the NKVD's headquarters, to file a complaint: Time has passed; where are my children? Before every visit to Lubianka he would say good-bye to everyone. He wrote several letters to Stalin in which he condemned the head of the NKVD. Then one day while going to get milk, he was waiting at the streetlight and somehow fell under a passing bread wagon. At the trial, the woman driver claimed that Dedya was bent over before lunging himself under the wheels—he must have been pushed violently. The official statement concluded that Dedya was intoxicated. The wretched NKVD idiots couldn't think of anything better. Dedya had never had a drop of alcohol.

I saw him off as best I could, by howling voicelessly in a dark corner in the hall, as though performing a ritual. I will never see you again; how can it be; I will never see you again, Dedya, my Dedya.

I felt that he could hear me.

Snowdrop

In fourth grade I followed around Svetlana Govorova, our star pupil. She embodied my unattainable ideal. She studied music. She could play Tchaikovsky.

My obsession had one practical goal: to get Govorova to play Tchaikovsky on the school's grand piano. How I adored Tchaikovsky! "Snowdrop," especially, but also "Troika," both from *The Seasons*. Govorova's stubby fingers danced over the keys, and I quivered like a bloodhound, staring over her shoulder at the music I couldn't read. But I could read the little poem by Maikov, printed on the same page, which I tried to sing along with her playing. Govorova objected, correctly, that "Snowdrop" wasn't a song to be sung, that the poem had nothing to do with the music, and when I tried to sing it anyway, she simply stopped playing. What torture it was to watch helplessly as she covered the keyboard, stood up, resettled her braids, smoothed down her dress, and sailed off without a glance!

My scheme to sing "Snowdrop" hinged on the word "rehearsal."

Our fourth grade was preparing for the end-of-the-year concert, and Govorova, our strongest musician, was recruited to accompany the singers. As the lead singer, I had a right to a rehearsal, so I kept dragging Govorova to the school auditorium, to the grand piano.

Others rehearsed there, too. My friend Natasha Korovina, along with the other athletes, was perfecting a so-called human pyramid, still very crooked. Larisa Moreva declaimed an excerpt from Gogol (she took declamation lessons at the Young Pioneers Palace; I despised her dreadful howling). I recited a French fable. The whole class screeched out "La Marseillaise," out of harmony. I can still remember the French words.

But I was crazy about Tchaikovsky, whose music, alas, was beyond my reach. I didn't attend a music school. There was no piano in my house. Forget the piano; my mother and I didn't even own a bed. Still, I persisted in my desire to sing "Snowdrop" to Govorova's accompaniment. But Govorova was a practical person. She ignored my threatening looks and handwritten notes. A class monitor and straight-A student, she occupied the central desk, a place of honor, which she shared with our second academic star, Mila, while I sat under the teacher's nose, together with the other outcasts. I failed every subject and never did any homework. F in math; F in history. Mama and I often didn't sleep. Some nights we had to walk in the street for hours, when Grandpa screamed particularly loudly. At school, everything was clean; the red floors sparkled; there were flowers in every window. At home, my mother and I slept on a mattress under a table, with the armies of bedbugs. That didn't stop me from dreaming about Tchaikovsky, but stubborn Govorova refused to play anything besides "Snowdrop," and she wouldn't let me sing.

Toward December the rehearsals intensified. I was now accompanied by the stately music teacher, who asked me what I wanted to sing. "Our Homeland Hears," I told her, though I wanted to say "Snowdrop." Very well. I trilled: "Our Homeland hears, / Our Homeland knows, / When one of her sons / In a plane swiftly goes."

I no longer slept in my grandfather's room on Chekhov Street: after several sleepless nights, Mama had rented a cot in Stoleshnikov Alley, in the apartment of a "respectable and sober" (the ad said) men's tailor. For centuries Stoleshnikov Alley had been Moscow's chief prostitution nest. Its families, from granny to granddaughter, plied their trade at night, crawling out like bedbugs. The Soviet government couldn't do anything, because officially prostitution didn't exist.

The tailor, his wife, and their son slept in a double bed by the wall, across from an enormous window of stained glass (before the revolution this must have been an artist's studio). Next to it, in a separate crib, slept their little daughter, who suffered from trachoma, a contagious disease that left her eyelids scarred and glued with pus. Mama and I shared a cot at the foot of the family bed, and I could see everything that went on in it. In the morning, the wife examined bloodied rags, muttering complaints about her husband.

Mama stayed at work until late. After school I returned to Stoleshnikov by myself.

The tailor's son, Yurka, was a little older than I was. His entrepreneurial mind was thinking up various business schemes. The girl stayed in her crib, quietly playing with a doll, occasionally looking at us through her scarred eyelids. The tailor—their

Stoleshnikov Alley in the late 1940s or early 1950s.

father—saw clients on Monday, took their measurements, very professionally, and received the fabric and a cash advance for the suit. Next, he immediately pawned the fabric and remained drunk until Wednesday; for the rest of the week he hid from his enraged clients, who demanded either the finished suit or the fabric and sometimes tried to break down the door with an ax. We were told not to open up.

The mother was in and out all day, visited often by a neighbor, the prostitute Lidka, who on seeing me enunciated, "Fourteen thousand." Beneath the unwashed window, in its fairy-tale light, they held whispered conversations and exchanged mysterious packages, always tightly wrapped, which must have contained drugs. Now and then a police patrol squad stomped in, received something from the wife, and stomped out. I was eleven or twelve that winter.

One afternoon, when no one was home, Yurka brought over a group of older kids: several boys and two girls. They all conferred excitedly and then proposed that I join them on an excursion to a nearby building. "You'll see," the girls promised me, "there are special birds up there—you'll see!"

I felt flattered: they had noticed me; they wanted my company!

We walked side by side in the street, holding hands, laughing and talking. It was a new, exciting life. I was seeing them for the first time, but it didn't matter—we would soon become fast friends, I thought, go to the movies together, to the skating rink, do all kinds of things together . . . No one had ever taken an interest in me before.

"Here! Bring her along! Let her see this, too!" the boys kept saying. Yurka's head bobbed among them.

They needed me!

We took a right on Petrovka Street and walked into the corner entrance behind the Red Poppy restaurant.

I saw a dark, narrow staircase. The boys crowded in front, not looking back, only laughing quietly. The girls closed ranks. One was clutching my hand; the other followed on my heels.

The boys reached the top floor and continued to climb.

"Almost there," the girl holding my hand reassured me.

"This way!" said the leading boy to the girl behind me. I let her pass. It was dark. The only light came from the attic. Someone was laughing up there. The other girl still held my hand. Suddenly I felt uncertain, even a little nauseated. Delicately I slipped my hand out of the girl's sweaty paw and scurried downstairs.

For some reason they didn't chase after me. They probably

hadn't worked it out yet, what to do in such cases. They let me escape.

It was already dark.

I couldn't go back to Stoleshnikov, so I walked over to Stanislavsky Street and hid in the building where my favorite teacher, Elizaveta Georgievna Orlova, lived with her husband, an army officer, and two sons. I sat outside her door for a long time. Luckily, no one saw me.

I returned to the tailor's at bedtime. Mama was waiting up for me. We ate, then crept into our cot. The family was sleeping in their communal bed. Yurka was lying quietly in his usual spot by the wall.

Like most children, I was afraid to share my secret fears with Mama. I just cried and begged her to return to Chekhov Street. I knew *they* wouldn't leave me alone.

I understood later that their tribe grew by initiating new females into the trade. Those two girls were also going to the attic for a reason.

Who was waiting for me there? A paying customer, that's who. Lidka wasn't spending time at the tailor's to chat about the weather. Fourteen thousand rubles was a huge sum then.

We left Stoleshnikov the next day, carrying our suitcase and blanket, like refugees. Arriving at the communal apartment where my grandfather lived, we rang the bell for a long time. Finally, one of the tenants, Misha Shilling, unbolted the door for us. Terrified of the other neighbors, we tiptoed down the hall and noiselessly pushed open the door to Grandpa's room.

Inside, it was dark and full of tobacco smoke. Grandpa was smoking shag in his torn armchair, spitting out occasionally.

He had been recently fired from everywhere. At night he bellowed and punched the wall with his fist. He had nothing to live on, nowhere to go.

Crouching under the table, we unrolled our blanket. Good to be home.

On New Year's Eve, in crisp brown ribbons (washed the night before and rolled wet around the hot water pipe), I sang proudly about the Homeland and her sons the aviators in front of the whole class.

Next, Govorova played "Snowdrop." I hid in the wings and sang softly, for the last time:

Early spring (antique postcard; detail).

A little blue snowdrop
In fragile spring snow—
The first dream of happiness
After a winter of sorrow.

I was choking on tears.
First dreams—that's what it was.
Our wretched lives.

The Wild Berries

A mother brought her girl to a boarding school for sickly children and then left. That girl was me.

The school stood over a large pond. All around it stretched an autumnal park with meadows and paths. Enormous trees seemed cast in gold and copper; the scent of fallen leaves made the girl dizzy, especially after the city's stench. The girl was in fact on a former gentleman's estate. The stately wooden manor had classical pillars, arched ceilings, and upper galleries; the girls' dormitory, called here a *dortoir*, was a former drawing room and featured a grand piano.

After the Socialist revolution, this building was going to be used by children with tuberculosis—children of the proletariat. It so happened that very soon, by the time the girl was in fifth grade, all Soviet citizens had become proletariat, lived in communal apartments, rode packed trams, and waited in line for a seat in public cafeterias. (They also waited for bread, potatoes, shoes, and, on rare occasions, a luxury item like a winter coat; in

This is 1948, soon after my return from the children's home. I'm wearing a new blouse with glass buttons! Mama plaited my hair and took me to the photo studio. But we are still homeless.

communal apartments, workers stood in line to use a bathroom, too.) A well-organized line meant fairness; one only had to wait long enough, and the girl had successfully waited for her turn at Forest School—that was the name of the facility.

I cannot describe the girl's appearance. Appearances cannot reveal inner life, and the girl, who was twelve at the time, led a constant inner monologue, making decisions literally each second—what to say, where to sit, how to answer—with a single purpose: to be like the other children, to avoid being kicked and shunned. But, at just twelve, the girl wasn't strong enough to watch her every step, to be at all times a model of neatness and moderation. She wasn't strong enough and so she'd run through the rainy autumnal park in torn stockings with her mouth open in an excited yelp, because, you see, they were playing hide-and-seek. (Between classes, too, she'd stampede the hallways, snot nosed, hair undone, always fighting; what a sight.)

At the boarding school, away from home, the girl was expected at the very least to keep track of her most necessary belongings, such as stockings: one was right there, by the bed, the other, God knows where. Handkerchiefs disappeared first, followed by her (right) mitten and scarf. As for pens, pencils, and erasers: a week into the school term no one in her class had theirs. Or take rubber boots: without them the girl couldn't walk through muddy puddles in the park nor enter the dining hall, and she lost one and now had to shuffle in her teacher's oversize castoff behind everyone in class, like a pariah.

That happened at the time when it was so important for the girl not to look worse than others, especially since there was this boy, Tolik—they were the same age but he was six inches shorter and of unspeakable beauty: a chiseled nose with freckles, endless thick eyelashes around starry eyes, plus a perpetual coy smirk. The girl was too tall for him, but this young god radiated his charm evenly and meaninglessly a hundred yards around like a tiny nuclear reactor. When he arrived in the dining hall the space around his table would light up and the girl felt a surge of merriment—Tolik's here!—and Tolik's eyes would grow larger as though under a magnifying glass as he scanned his kingdom. Heads turned to him like sunflowers to the sun, thought the girl, stabbed in her very heart. There was a swelling right above it, the size of a young wild berry. Every child at Forest School had such swellings. Once, the girl was presented with a heavenly vision of Tolik, who'd just walked in and was immediately jostled by another boy. "Watch out for my breasts, moron," Tolik whimpered clownishly. His hand was cupped over his left nipple. Him, too! the girl cried out silently. His breasts hurt, too, not just mine, not just the girls'! He's one of us—we're going through the same stage, together. The girl shuffled into the dining hall—always the last one, kept back by the infernal boot.

In a commune no one is entitled to private meals; it's considered hoarding. Everything must be shared with other children, even poor biscuits from home. After a childhood of collective care the girl had lost her sense of privacy and individual property. The commune also dislikes when one of them acts differently: always comes late or wears mismatched boots. The girl became an outcast in her class. She began to fall behind on purpose, to avoid scornful looks, and one October night at the end of the second week she fell so far behind the other girls that she found herself alone among the boys. Dark shadows blocked her path, cutting her off from the girls and their teacher far ahead, pulling her in a circle the way a pack of wolves pulls in its prey.

I stood surrounded on the edge of the park. The other girls, protected and safe, were barely visible now.

I screamed after them. I bellowed like a tuba, like a siren.

The boys nearest to me grinned stupidly. (Later, in my grown life, I'd always recognize that dumb, dirty smirk, a companion to base, dirty deeds.) Their arms were wide open, ready to grab me. Their fingers were moving and their wild berries probably hardened at that moment. I stood still, directing my scream at the girls; some of them looked back and continued to walk away, faster. I kept increasing the volume.

What would they do to me?

They'd have to tear me to pieces and bury the remains of their chase, but only after they were finished doing all that could be done to a living person who'd become someone's property.

But for now they just wanted me to shut up.

Something made them pause when they were only five feet away. I hurled myself through their ring and flew across the meadow, losing my boot in the mud. At the door I overtook the last of the girls. She heard me thumping and looked around: on her face I saw the same dirty, complicit smirk. I tumbled inside. I was red and swollen from crying but wasn't asked a single question as to what might have caused all that yelling back in the park. Those girls knew what had lain in store for me, somehow. Maybe they'd all shared a past in the caves, where their female ancestors were chased down and used. (How quickly can children regress to a primitive life, accept its simple truths! Common fire and women; collective meals shared equally: the leaders get more, the weak get less or nothing. Sleep together on a filthy floor; grab food from a single pile; pass around a cigarette butt; not be disgusted with others' fluids; dress in identical rags . . .)

That night the girls were quiet in a strange, contented way, as though their hunger for justice had been sated. They didn't know yet that I'd escaped. What would they do if I had come back alive but broken, soiled?

The word for such a person was "excreted." The girl knew excreted kids in her schoolyard. The excreted were up for grabs, outside the commune—anyone could abuse them in any way they wanted. The thing to do was to stalk them everywhere they went and then slam them into a wall in plain view. All excreted had the look of dumb cattle; two or three stalkers always tailed them. Only constant adult presence could have saved them from abuse, but one can't expect adult presence on each path, on each corner.

The next day was like any other. I fished my boot out of the mud and tried to hobble livelier. The boys greeted me as always (slugged on the neck, shoved into a puddle), while other girls were watching like hawks for anything out of the ordinary. But no one hollered, no one pointed fingers at me, and eventually it became clear that nothing had happened: I must have escaped. Things went back to normal.

Only one person at the sanatorium, Tolik, sensed that something had in fact happened. Tolik was a prime chaser: his hunter's instincts were by far the sharpest in the pack. He began stalking me. In dark corners his starry eyes frisked my body while his buddies guarded the perimeter glumly, not sharing his smirk: this chase wasn't theirs. It wasn't courtship, it was something else, something the girls couldn't find a name for and only shrugged their shoulders at. I alone understood that Tolik followed the whiff of shame still clinging to me.

Other kids left the girl alone: she'd won her place in the sun, so to speak, with her powerful lungs and refusal to cave in. It turned out that she was blessed with an exceptionally strong voice—she could bellow as low as a hippo and as high as a drunken cat—and that newfound talent would kick in at a moment of danger. In addition, she'd pushed herself academically, and it mattered at Forest School, which wasn't just any public summer camp where a child was measured by her ability to get up on time. Good grades were considered an honest achievement here—you couldn't get an A by punching noses—and if a teacher read your composition in front of the class, that wasn't something to sneer at.

I'd mainly spent my childhood waiting in line at public cafeterias and in our communal apartment's kitchen, where academic excellence didn't matter to my survival. Now, pitted against a hostile tribe, I feverishly applied myself to writing a composition about autumn. My final draft piled azure skies upon turquoise dusk, bronze upon gold, and crystals upon corals, so the astonished teacher—a consumptive beauty in an orthopedic corset—passed my opus around to the other teachers and then read it out loud to the entire class—the same class that had nearly destroyed me.

I followed up with verse for the school paper's special edition, in honor of Constitution Day. It wasn't real poetry, of course, the kind that spills out of a dying person like blood and becomes the stuff of ruthless jokes. No, my creation was beyond mockery and could only bring respect. The Soviet people are the strongest in the world, it went, and they want peace for every nation—six lines in all. "Your own work?" the beautiful teacher inquired, and her corset squeaked.

A new pair of rubber boots arrived from home. In the electric light of the girls' latrine, at night, I memorized spelling rules. My new powerful voice was now part of the school choir and I was chosen to dance, too, in a swift Moldavian circle dance—the school was preparing the New Year's program. Then we were to go home.

That meant never again would I see my tormentor, my Tolik—your name is like sweet warm milk; your face shines over me like a sun; your eyes are full of indolence and lust.

In the dark corners Tolik showered me with obscenities loudly and clearly. Six inches shorter but straight and firm as an arrow: a high-strung consumptive boy keen on his target. Everyone at school became used to the sight of a tall girl splayed between Tolik's arms. Each night I dreamed of his face.

The girl pulled on her new boots and slowly walked through the snowy park to meet her mother—her time in paradise was up; they were going home. At the winter palace, among crystals and corals of frozen trees, Tolik was living through the final hours of his reign.

This was after the New Year's concert, where I performed solo in front of the choir, then swirled in a wild Moldavian circle dance. (For you alone, my Tolik.) Tolik performed, too: it turned out he had a beautiful, clear soprano and he delivered a song about Soviet Motherland and her brave sons the aviators to the accompaniment of a grand piano. He was visibly nervous and the absence of his cynical smirk was so striking that people clapped uncertainly, surprised at their king's concern with his audience.

Then there was dinner, followed by the main attraction: a formal dance. In the early 1950s children were taught the orderly dances of the aristocratic finishing schools—polonaise, pas de quatre, pas d'Espagne—and now a slow pas de quatre was announced, ladies ask gentlemen. Tolik had recovered from his stage fright and was exchanging smirks, directed at me, with his entourage. I walked up to him. Our icy fingers entwined and we curtsied and bowed woodenly across the floor. Tolik was thrown off track by my public sniffling and didn't even crack jokes. Instead, after the dance, he respectfully walked me over to my nook behind a pillar. I retired to the *dortoir* and wept there until the girls returned. There was no more ambiguity, no more heady interrogations in dark corners: Tolik clearly didn't know what to do with me anymore.

I was picked up last, as always. We crawled along the white highway, under dark skies, dragging my poor suitcase. The *dortoir* windows were throwing farewell lights on the snowy road.

I never saw Tolik again, but I heard his silvery voice on the phone. He called me at home, in Moscow.

My grandfather's daughter from his second marriage, who occupied the next room in our communal apartment, yelled that I must come to the phone. "For you," she announced with her customary bug-eyed look. "Some guy."

"What guy—there's no guy . . . Hello?"

"It's Tolik, remember?" the high voice sang out.

"Oh, it's you, Lena," I said, greeting Tolik, with a significant glance at the daughter and my mother, who'd also come into the hall. "It's Lena Mitiaieva from school, Mom."

Uncle Misha, unmarried and a radiologist at the KGB clinic, decided to join the party and now stood in his blue army long johns between the black draperies of his doorway. The apartment's entire population was now in the hall, minus the Kalinovskys, minus my grandfather's second wife, minus my grandfather, who was smoking shag in bed, minus the janitor, Aunt Katya.

The idea was that everyone was waiting to use the phone.

"It's me, Tolik," continued the voice.

"No, Lena, I can't tonight—they are going to the movies, Mom"—an aside to my mother.

"What movies—it's late," my mother answered quickly, while Uncle Misha and the daughter seemed to be waiting for more.

My love, my holiest secret, was calling me and I had to speak to him in front of everybody!

"No, Lena, why?" I kept repeating vaguely, because Tolik on the other end was persistently inviting me to join him right away at the Grand Illusion for a movie. I was in a mental swoon and kept on mumbling nonsense for my listeners' benefit. The listeners had guessed the truth, of course, and now wanted to see me squirm.

Azure skies, turquoise dusk, pas de quatre, my tears, his icy fingers all vanished, and remained in paradise. Here was another story—here I was a fifth-grader with a chronic cold and torn brown stockings. The world of crystals and corals, of miraculous deliveries, of undying love—that world couldn't coexist with the communal apartment and my grandfather's room in particular, full of books and bedbugs, where my mother and I (officially homeless) were allowed to sleep in a corner under his desk. My Tolik, my little prince, my dauphin couldn't possibly be standing in a dark, stinking phone booth near the grimy Grand Illusion.

I didn't believe Tolik, and rightly so, for I could hear coarse voices in the background and hoots of laughter. Again, the circle of dirty smirks was tightening. But this time I was far away.

"Neighbors want the phone," I concluded indifferently (choking back tears). "'Bye, Lena."

Tolik called again after that, inviting me to go skating or to see a movie. "No, Lena, why?" I mumbled miserably. "What do you mean, why?" giggled back shameless Tolik.

Clearly Tolik, that prime chaser, had figured out how to use my unhappy love for his dark purposes. But—the circle of animal faces had never crushed the girl; it remained behind, among the tall trees of the park, in the enchanted kingdom of wild berries.

Gorilla

Nobody noticed her—she was just a skinny kid, kicking the ball with the neighborhood boys. Girls from the good families, the beautiful Albina, Olga, and her sister Irina, were gathering their bloom quietly, with dignity. They lived in the two-story house behind the little girl's apartment building. A murder took place in that house some years before, a man was killed; some said it was Albina's father. He opened the door, apparently, to a stranger, and was shot. The rear house was famous for its endless cellar believed to run across Chekhov Street, but no one was brave enough to check, except for the little girl.

Among the children in the courtyard was Shchenik, a handsome boy who went to a music school and always carried around his accordion. He sported little sideburns and almost a pompadour, like the future Elvis Presley. But the little girl ignored him and played in the dust obliviously, and the only young man she was in contact with, and tried to avoid, was the scary Garik, nicknamed Gorilla, who always wanted to push her, to grab her, to twist her braids. Once when, sweaty and out of breath from playing, she waited for the elevator, it happened: Gorilla swept in, grabbed the girl, and dragged her into the operator's little nook, empty for the day. He kept pressing her into the wall with his body, while the girl bleated, "Mama, Mama," but her mama was waiting upstairs; she couldn't hear the bleating through the four massive floors.

"Mama, Mama, Mama!"

"Coming, sweetie, I'm right here!"

Suddenly, a glimpse of the dear face, Mama was running toward her, and Gorilla evaporated. Mama! How could she know? How could she hear? How could she run four flights in three seconds? She couldn't. She must have watched from the window, seen the girl, seen Gorilla, understood everything, and started running.

Such was the charming company the girl kept until the grown children were ready to leave their nest, their courtyard. Some were destined to move up in this life, some to move down, and some to remain forever in their old courtyard, to come back there every night from work and raise their own children there.

In the summer, the girl played *lapta* in the courtyard, and in the winter went to the Dinamo skating rink, where a creep with golden tooth caps sidled up to her one evening and wouldn't leave her alone. She switched to the TDK rink, but when she was waiting there for a ticket in a large crowd, the crowd suddenly swayed, and someone yanked on the skates she was holding and disappeared. In tears, the girl shuffled over to the police station, accompanied by a friend, the janitor's daughter Nina, to report the theft. There they told her to come back a week later, which she did, again with Nina. The tired officer looked at her, looked at Nina, and produced a pair of beaten skates: "There, your skates have been found."

"But these are not mine!"

"No? Then look for yours in here."

And he unlocked a huge cabinet packed floor to ceiling with skates. The girl went through every shelf, but didn't find hers. A catastrophe. Her mother had scraped to buy those skates; she'd never afford a new pair. She began to weep; the officer lost patience: "Just take what you want!" He needed to close her file. Dying from guilt, the girl grabbed a pair of skates a size too big and skated in them until college.

Later she understood that the cabinet contained confiscated loot: she could have chosen the best pair, and all thanks to Nina, whom every policeman treated like his own, because janitors and police are brothers and sisters. Besides, Nina was such a lovely, diligent, well-spoken child that everyone listened to her and welcomed her. It was so easy to be friends with Nina: one could just drop in on her anytime; hers was the only family in the courtyard that permitted it. They all lived in a single room, in the basement, at the end of a dirty-pink corridor so narrow two people couldn't pass each other. In that room she lived with her mother, Granya, the building's janitor; Granya's boyfriend, Ivanov, a bandit; and their four-month-old daughter. The girl was on her way to call on Nina as usual, when the other janitor, a Tatar named Raya, stopped her in that horrible corridor and told her sternly not to go in there, to stay away, and quickly left.

The girl stepped into Nina's room, which was empty, except for the baby, who was lying naked on the table, kicking her feet.

The floor in the room was wet. The girl sensed that something had happened in that room. Later, because nothing remained secret in the courtyard, the girl found out that the drunken Ivanov had raped Nina, who was fourteen. Granya didn't go to the police right away; she waited; and then she went and reported that Ivanov kept a steel rod under his pillow and threatened to kill them all. It probably was true; Ivanov must have felt cramped living in the same room with Nina, but there was nowhere to go. Janitors and police are brothers and sisters, so Ivanov was arrested and sent to jail for a year, for now, but then what? They couldn't just let him go, they all knew what he was really in for. So he was shanked right before his year was up; such was the price for Nina. A man went to jail for one thing, got executed for another, something that couldn't be voiced in court out of respect for the victim.

In the spring, the puddles dried out, the girls changed into socks, the old lime tree disappeared under the fragrant yellow fuzz, the smells of new grass and leaves filled the courtyard, and in the evenings, the little garden behind the two-story house rippled with the sound of Shchenik's accordion.

There, underneath the trees, the beautiful Albina, Olga, and Irina, the unapproachable daughters of good families, laughed coquettishly. Somebody's cigarette glowed (whose?), and the accordion sang its nightingale song.

And one night, dressed in her best, with her mother's gauzy scarf over her shoulders, with a beating heart the girl descended from her fourth floor and with a new, graceful step glided across the courtyard into the little garden, where the cigarette glowed and laughter was ringing. Happiness awaited her there, she knew.

They all turned around when she approached.

With her newfound grace, the girl calmly joined their circle, and they made room for her, respectfully, as if for a young lady, their peer. They didn't chase her away or laugh her off.

Shchenik began to play, someone's tossed cigarette flickered in the dark, and a young man, tall, in a gray suit, stepped out from the deep shadow. He offered the girl his hand, inviting her to dance. Her heart stopped—a prince! A prince from the magical dusky kingdom! She lifted her eyes.

It was Gorilla.

He stood easily next to the girl, as if he had some right to her. So, in the transparent spring air, among the aromas of new leaves and grass, to the sweet song of the accordion, she was supposed to enjoy the sight of this Gorilla? *He* was the promised happiness of her first spring?

His hand continued to hang limply between them.

"Beat it, you moron," the girl said automatically. "Idiot."

Gorilla smiled his stupid smile at her, his hand still hanging.

So the girl turned on her heel and marched back to her building and never again returned to that little corner of earth where, to the music of streetcars and accordion, every Saturday the mystery of passing from childhood into youth took place. All spring, every Saturday, the girl's heart fluttered at the music, but she was angry and refused to come out.

And in the fall Gorilla disappeared. The inscription "Gorilla is a looney," scratched next to his front door, survived him, and over many years faded slowly under the Moscow rain, snow, and wind. As the courtyard rumor told it, Gorilla had found some piece of equipment, somewhere, brought it home, tried it; it made him ill; he was hospitalized.

There are so many boys like him—boys who need to try everything, to blow everything up, to throw things into the fire, just to see what happens, to pursue and to hunt, to catch and to take away, to pull everything apart. Like many of them, Gorilla remained forever in his childhood. The girl cried and cried watching from her window the little bus and Gorilla, in his gray suit, under the falling snow, beneath the white shroud, in a coffin resting on kitchen chairs, with hands crossed, like a grown-up, Gorilla, Gorilla.

Moscow Courtyard by Sergei V. Volkov (1989).

Dying Swan

My mother adored poetry. When my sixth-grade Russian teacher, nicknamed Dying Swan, gave us an assignment to compose a poem at home, my mother lit up. She kept me awake half the night—we were looking for a rhyme for "barefoot." In the morning I copied the poem into a notebook, under Mama's supervision, and submitted it to Dying Swan. I almost never did any homework, was a failing student, and always sat in the front row, under the teacher's nose.

A day later the triumphant Swan arrived to class, frothing with malice like a fire extinguisher. Leaning her voluminous hip against my desk, she expounded for the next forty-five minutes on the subject of theft, repeating the word "plagiarism," then unknown to us.

My head was almost touching her permanently undone zipper. Poor old Swan was a weird lady. She dyed her hair orange, but always did it wrong: her hair remained dirty white, but her scalp turned bright red, like an Iroquois in an old painting. For some reason she hated our class intensely.

I stared mindlessly at her swaying belly folds, simultaneously composing with my deskmate a mocking ode about our crocodile of a zoology teacher, who, the day before, had made us study intestinal parasites, plunking little jars with preserved tapeworms right onto our desks. I ran out of the room, sick, and didn't come back, for which I received an F; now I was sublimating my rightful vengeance into art.

Swan's tirade was interrupted by the bell. After class I approached Swan innocently and asked if she had liked my poem. She gave me a crazed look and screamed that it was about me she had just talked for an hour, about my theft! "You stole your so-called poem from the poet Agnia Barto! It's called plagiarism!" She stormed out, shaking the class ledger, and I was left with another F, in literature.

The poem Mama and I had composed went like this:

All is quiet in the flat,
Kids are sleeping, sleeps the cat.
Only Tanya sits in bed.

The subject was September 1, the first day of school. And the ending:

Little Tommy sleeps alone
In the attic, barefoot.
He is black; he's not white folk;
And below him sleeps New York.

In my imagination I could see that poor black American boy, pitiful to the point of tears, who sleeps in the attic of a New York skyscraper, so oppressed by capitalists that he doesn't even attend school.

Sanych

Today I can admit that I loved him. I loved and worshipped my teacher like a deity.

Rather short, always grumpy, and with a ruddy complexion and eyes almost without color, Aleksandr A. Plastinin, "Sanych," taught literature in the final grade, which meant Soviet classics like Gorky, Fadeev, Ostrovsky—unreadable rubbish. Teaching that material must have been a daily torment for him. But he was assigned to teach the final grade, and this was his curriculum.

Our two neighborhood schools, Women's PS 635 and Men's PS 170, where Sanych had always taught, were separated by an iron fence seven feet tall. It was like a magnet for both populations. On our side, on spring days, girls jumped rope, played awkward girlish volleyball, and sat around on benches, laughing deliberately loudly, transmitting scorn. From the other side came thundering sounds of an intense soccer game, hushed swearing and shuffling over the pavement during fistfights, followed by full-voiced threats and insults as both sides walked away. Across the street from the men's school stood Vysokopetrovsky Monastery, where in complete devastation I discovered the tombstone of Natalia Kirillovna Naryshkina, the mother of Peter the Great. (It was at that defiled tombstone that I fell in love with the Russian royal names Natalia, Kirill, and Peter and decided to give them to my future children. That came to pass.) On the other side of Moskvin Street stood the gypsy theater Romen; a notorious police station, later disbanded for some serious misdoings; and the Musical Theatre. That was the Moscow of 1954, which had just buried Stalin.

Right before my senior year it was decided that the two schools would merge. A group of girls, including myself, was exiled to PS 170 from their native PS 635, with its polished dark floors, shiny windows, and dear old teachers. Discipline reigned there, too, but it was the discipline of an army barracks. Generations of juvenile bandits from Pushkin and Petrovka Streets, Stoleshnikov and Degtiarny Alleys, had marked the school walls with indelible smells, like tomcats. The school stank like a menagerie, if animals could smoke. When I read the names of the girls who were being transferred there, I crawled home, shaking with tears.

In my new co-ed class, fifty percent of the students brayed, spat at long distance, looked insolently with unfocused eyes, wore army crew cuts, chewed their nails, and had great difficulty speaking without swearing. In the evenings some of them walked to the military barracks to fight with soldiers. The other fifty percent adorned their uniforms with white lace, wore long braids, read Dreiser, Balzac, and Romain Rolland, attempted to wear bangs, and believed that not a single kiss should be given without love (not that anyone asked). Their speech consisted of phrases like "the White Army suffered a fiasco."

To this ridiculous hybrid Sanych was supposed to present the monumental Soviet classic *Mother*, by Maxim Gorky. Naturally he couldn't have despised us more.

The very first day he forbade the use of ballpoint pens (some rich students already owned them). In his classroom everyone was equal and had to use standard metal quills and inkwells. Soon one student, Voinov, fell victim to this policy. Sanych noticed in his hand an expensive foreign-made pen; he swiftly yanked it from Voinov's petrified fingers, broke it in two, and tossed it out an open window. Then he returned to his notebook.

Sanych owned a thick, well-used notebook, from which he recited monotonously everything we needed to know. We were required to write after him at maximum speed. He never improvised, never digressed, never joked. How could he joke, poor thing, with Gorky's *Mother* on the table?

Other teachers allowed themselves a little merriment. Arriving to class, the unforgettable physics instructor Nikolai Semenovich, nicknamed One-Twenty for his limp, announced in a rusty voice: "Attention! Hang your ears on a nail! Dynamo—is—a—force—that . . ." This is the only thing I still remember from the multiyear physics course.

The math teacher Ilya Nikolaevich referred fondly to "h little and H gigantic."

Each teacher had his or her favorite method of handling the class. The drafting instructor Proegorkin shrieked over the buzzing noise. The chemistry teacher Colba, a heavy, clever, and sickly woman, issued vitriolic comments and lots of Fs.

As for Sanych, he spewed his lectures like automatic gunfire, drilling our heads with his colorless, wide-open eyes. One couldn't get distracted for a moment. He never shouted or raised his already loud voice. With the belligerent intonation normally used for sarcastic polemics, he imparted neutral facts about the author, the history of the book, its main characteristics, and so on.

Sanych's anger was caused by his own helplessness in the face of the boys' insurmountable idiocy and the girls' feminine cretinism. As if the boys weren't bad enough, for the first time in his distinguished career he faced at the blackboard all those ribbons, curls, braids, pinafores, stockings, giggles, stupefied teary eyes, and squeaky, cowardly bleating.

How bitterly he mocked our early-developed Lenka (D-size cups, sweaty underarms, mustache, enormous calves) when she squeezed out a garbled "Saaantimentalism." He, the leading teacher of the men's lyceum, had to listen to this nonsense! "'Saaantimentalism'!"

Later I understood that his raised intonation, monotonous and threatening, stimulated our nerves, already tense. It was an expression of his powerful will as an educator. His lectures were a baleful outburst, devoid of any playfulness. To play before *this* audience?

On judgment days, at the end of each topic, Sanych took care of us efficiently. He cleared the first six desks and called the first six victims with their pens and notebooks. They were to write their answers, which he graded on the spot. Two more wrote on the board. Another pupil took the hot spot at the teacher's table for oral questioning. If he couldn't answer, the rest of us were called.

It was a scene of mass execution. Pauses between stammering answers were filled with timid rustling of the chalk on the board and quills on paper. Grades rained into the class ledger. In forty-five minutes he examined twenty students, half the class (he had forty-two). His white eyes frisked the rows of desks.

He was named the best teacher in the district, and the leading theorist; college students sat in on his lectures, bringing their own chairs.

Nothing matched the terror of our worst delinquents in his class. Those cropped heads and cigarette-sucking mugs, those paws covered with warts, more used to fistfights than to spelling, actually tried to read and write under Sanych's ferocious onslaught. To speak without swearwords. To express their thoughts in compositions. To write after him in their scraggly hands. They sweated during his interrogations.

"Gorky was born . . . was born . . . in, like . . ." A silent appeal to the timid masses. "He was born in, like, eighteen hundred . . ."

"Naturally he was born after eighteen hundred. He wasn't born in the eighteenth century, was he?"

The class brays obediently.

"Eighteen sixty-eight!"

"Incredible. Now. When was the novel *Mother* written?"

"In, like, nineteen hundred . . ."

"Think. You are aiming at a firm C."

". . . Oh-five!"

"Sit down. F. Seriakov!"

"Oh-seven!"

"Close enough. Come to the blackboard."

The recipient of the F bleats mournfully: "Aleksandr Sanych, I studied . . ."

"So you'll study some more. Koneva, if you prompt him again, you'll get an F, too."

It was like a game of fortune.

I got hooked very quickly. His condescension was irresistible bait. Everything he assigned I had read a long time before. Gorky's *Mother* annoyed me vaguely, as did all of Gorky's big novels and plays, all those *Klim Samgin*, *Foma Gordeev*, *The Zykovs*. I enjoyed his *Childhood*, "Out and About," his gypsy tales. The famous "The sea—was laughing" touched a nerve. On the one hand, this was against all grammar rules. On the other, it opened up new stylistic perspectives. And that strange em dash.

Since childhood I'd been addicted to reading. At home I was always buried in a book; I ruined my eyes that way. And now I was being ignored by a literature teacher!

I felt he ignored me on purpose. He never looked at my raised hand. Maybe he thought I was a nerd, a teacher's pet. Glasses, braids. Fresh voice. He didn't know that back at my old school I was the worst pupil, nothing but Ds and Fs, plus terrible discipline marks, always sitting in the front row under the teacher's nose. But at the men's school I didn't have a reputation yet, so I was allowed to sit in the back. I was sixteen, a grown young person with a rich inner world and an acute sense of justice. I even managed to study better, out of pride. Even in algebra, the horror of my life.

There we were, a proud girl in braids and lace and a white-eyed drill sergeant. I remember his first written assignment, a composition about Gorky's *Mother*. I didn't have time to reread the cursed novel. I had glanced through it ages before, at the library, or maybe Mama had bought it. Mama kept buying books

High school yearbook, 1956. Myself and Aleksandr A. Plastinin (Sanych), my favorite teacher.

maniacally—her entire family library had perished during the arrests—and I kept reading them. After school I always went to the library instead of home, where nothing good awaited me. The librarians took advantage of my addiction, and for every two books I requested, they forced me to read at least one on the school curriculum. Gorky's *Mother* must have been one of the compulsory items.

Only one scene stuck in my memory. It is dark, the factory whistle blows, and the villagers are getting ready to leave for work. The doors open, and the light from the huts falls on the fat mud of the road. Around this tableau I built my composition, which I made sound like the beginning of the later masterpiece *One Day in the Life of Ivan Denisovich.*

But, if you think about it, what light could be falling on that road? They had only candles back then, and the front doors of Russian peasant huts led not into the house itself but into the unlit and unheated anteroom, the so-called dark room. No light could be coming from there.

I also remember another line: "A blind, deaf, breast-sucking despair." Like Helen Keller in infancy.

I wrote in a tight hand, in a graphed notebook, on each line. My composition was short. A challenge to fate cannot be long-winded.

He accepted my challenge. He gave me a B+ and commented in red pencil. At the next class he smiled, very faintly, or so I thought. And he looked just a little bit pleased.

I didn't need much. My sails filled with wind. I raced ahead, newly in love with myself.

A tiny phrase of his, and I'm repeating it all day. Interpreting it this way and that. "Original but arguable."

On the next judgment day he summons me to the front desk and I quickly write an answer. Briefly and unconventionally, the way he prefers. He reads it on the spot, quietly asks me an additional question. I object to his objection. He nods, surprised, then smiles. We have a conspiracy.

I'm dizzy. It's like first love. Youngsters fall in love with anyone who pays them the slightest attention.

My self-esteem shoots through the roof. I want to improve myself. I receive another B+. Good enough, for now.

I've become his best student. Later I learn that in every class he has a best student. In the ninth grade it's Sulimova, a proud-looking girl in pretty yellow shoes. I look at her in disbelief: It cannot be. There cannot be two of us. (There are many of us, it turns out.)

It's spring, the final exam—composition. I'm nervous and can't finish proofreading; the bell has already rung. Everyone is leaving. Sanych is at his table and suddenly he says, "Don't rush. Take as long as you need."

We remain in the empty classroom for a long time, me and my love. As I'm leaving he says, "I'll proofread it, too."

For the final composition I receive an A. My last A from Sanych. From then on I would always write compactly, in graphed notebooks, on every line. The way he taught me.

I saw him once more. A year later we had a reunion. The former pupils were partying, laughing, singing, joking, celebrating our friendship, our common past. It was February 1957. Suddenly I discovered many intelligent, enlightened faces among the boys from the previous years.

A small vortex in the foyer, and in its center a gray head, a ruddy face, and very light eyes. Sanych. He is laughing shyly. I hear shouts: "Sanych, Sanych." The boys must have shared a drink with him. They address him tenderly, but without familiarity. It is now clear who was everyone's favorite teacher. They won't let him go. A whole crowd follows him out.

Later I learned that one sees colorless eyes like his in people suffering from heart disease.

Many years later I was being feted at the German embassy in Moscow: I had been awarded the Pushkin Prize. There were several of us chatting in a circle: the writer Anatoly Makarov, the painter Boris Messerer, the economist and author Nikolai Shmelev. Suddenly we discovered that we all had graduated from the same high school, PS 170, and that we all shared a teacher, Aleksandr Sanych Plastinin.

"Sanych died young," I told them. "He wasn't forty-eight. According to legend, he fathered eight children. Then he married a former pupil. She had graduated from our school and stayed there as a lab assistant. She had been in love with him since childhood. She loved him very deeply. She was a cousin of my classmate Mila. She gave him more children. They lived in great poverty. End of legend." My male companions paused respectfully and then began to talk about Sanych, about the role he had played in their lives. We decided to establish an association of Sanych's former students. Then we all went home.

Sanych is in his grave. He has been dead for many years.

"The doors open, and the light from the huts falls on the fat mud of the road."

Foundling

I was discovered among the virgin lands of Kazakhstan. The people who found me were Konstantin Ardi and Vasily Ananchenko, Moscow correspondents of *The Late Night News*, a daily radio program. Later, when I began working there, this became my nickname: Foundling.

To be precise, they found me at the radio station in Petropavlovsk, the capital of northern Kazakhstan. Ardi and Ananchenko came to Petropavlovsk to work on a story, and I arrived there from the provincial town of Bulaevo to retrieve the typesetting for my newsletter—I was responsible for producing a newsletter about the work of Moscow State University's student brigade.

It was September. All students had returned to Moscow, tanned and emaciated, equipped with songs, wages, and biscuits, dressed in striped sailor sweatshirts and duck trousers, a donation from the navy. They were leaving behind giant silos, built with native stone, adobe houses, and sheds for sheep. Those buildings were supposed to be finished by seasonal workers from Armenia, but I don't know if anyone ever finished them or if they were buried under the snow after the campaign to familiarize college students with the simple life of prison laborers was over.

Also, they left me—I had to finish the newsletter, which I wrote myself under different names.

But then a radio editor in Petropavlovsk belatedly decided to put out a story about our brigade. He called the Bulaevo Party Committee office, where I was staying alone with my guitar. Oh, the nights in the deep Kazakh province! An empty office with a cot; a phone in the hallway; dogs barking in every yard; not a single light anywhere. Then the phone rings. Who can be calling so late?

"Miss, is anyone from the student brigade still around?"

"Everyone's gone."

"But what about you?"

"I'm working on the brigade's newsletter. It's almost done."

"You are exactly who I need! Can you come to Petropavlovsk to talk on our radio program? I was away and missed them. I wanted to record them at work, singing at the bonfire . . ."

"Actually I was going to Petropavlovsk tomorrow, to collect the typeset for the newsletter. And I happen to own a guitar."

Pause. The editor is digesting this amazing coincidence.

"Well. You are welcome to stay at my house. My wife will cook a meal."

Fat snowflakes twirled over the one-story town of Bulaevo; vast puddles rippled like oceans in a storm. A strong, early winter wind was blowing from the steppes. I was winding my way to the station, dragging my guitar. By way of clothes I had a red raincoat, made in China, and an orange kerchief that resembled a waffled towel. Underneath I wore a sailor sweatshirt, bell-bottomed duck trousers, and green army boots. Everything, except for the navy surplus garments, was purchased by my poor mother. I shed tears over those purchases but wore them anyway. That was my wardrobe when I headed for the virgin lands in the early summer, toward my fate.

*   *   *

This is how I ended up there.

That spring, at the end of my senior year in the department of journalism, I made an attempt to find a job. I tried the weekly publication *The Week*, where my contact, a former classmate, sent me hints by opening a desk drawer with an empty cognac bottle—but I don't give bribes, on principle; I tried the satirical publication *The Crocodile*, where another of my classmates had been hired. I tried the radio, the satire and humor department, where the correspondents laughed politely when I stumbled in from the street, announcing that I wanted to work there. The reason I looked for work in humor-related offices was my freshly minted diploma. My specialty was humor pieces and short satirical sketches. But I couldn't get a position.

At this difficult point in my career I heard that the university was sending a student brigade somewhere to Kazakhstan, to conquer the virgin lands. So I devised a plan: I would travel across the country with that brigade. When else would I get a chance to see Kazakhstan? That was the spirit of the time. Difficulties at home? Pack up and go across the Urals, to the end of the world.

•   •   •

To be honest, the crucial stage of my education, the final oral exam, I approached with zero enthusiasm or effort. It happens to students at the end of senior year. I stopped studying. My senior thesis, "On the Nature of Humor," I cobbled together at the last moment, the night before the deadline. It consisted of twelve pages of theory and a dozen freelance pieces I had written as an intern for *The Crocodile*. At the defense, the committee members were trying to decide whether my jokes were funny. Eventually

Summer of 1958. During my internship with *Sovetskaia molodezh* in Jurmala, Latvia. I even applied some lipstick, which always bounced around in my purse but was never used.

they reconciled, and I got a B+ and departed quite pleased with myself.

During my five years of studies I not only learned nothing new but actually forgot what I used to know in high school. In the journalism department they were turning out future ideologues, first and foremost. We had to read endless tomes on the Communist press, primarily by Lenin. Then there were courses in dialectic materialism, historical materialism, the foundations of Marxist philosophy, some ridiculous empirical criticism, also by Lenin, interspersed with sporadic attempts to instill in us correct spelling and basic editing principles. Our class included stars of local journalism from the Soviet Union's many republics, whose knowledge of the imperial language was more than shaky. In the one-page dictations, some students made thirty or more mistakes—the record was thirty-eight, by a student from Baku. They went on to become editors in chief of their local papers. In addition, we had among us two unhurried Mongolian students who in five years failed to take notes on a single lecture.

To teach someone to speak correctly is almost impossible. It's easier to teach a foreigner, who will simply memorize the rules. A native-speaking provincial whose conversational Russian had been ruined from birth by the illiterate speech of the lumpen industrial outskirts couldn't be taught in principle, despite the presence of brilliant instructors. In any case, the department's main concern was to instill in us faithful interpretations of the Party dogmas. We were being trained to become ideologically sound ignoramuses, despite the availability of an outstanding classical literature.

Only the final exam stood between me and graduation:

"Theory and Practice of the Soviet Party Press and the Foreign Communist Press." God. I couldn't force myself to cram for this. The night before the exam I pulled myself together and decided to walk over to the library to glance through the encyclopedia. I didn't know a single name, a single date, nothing.

Unfortunately, fate sent Yurka, my classmate, and his mother to intercept me while I was crawling, full of doubt, to the unknown source of information concerning the foreign Communist press. (Our dear professors had never bothered to put together a textbook on this mysterious subject.)

Junior year. At the humor magazine *The Crocodile*.

"Hi," shouted Yurka, "it's my birthday, come with us!" His petite mother, a radiologist, beamed at me. "Why not," I responded irresponsibly. I returned home on the last train.

In the morning I was understandably late for the exam. My exhausted classmates were crowded at the door, staring at their notebooks with unseeing eyes. It was too late to borrow their notes. They themselves must have begged the class nerds. The A students were already in the auditorium.

I peeked in. *Mamma mia.* Not bad for a state-appointed committee. I saw the one-armed departmental chair, plus young Zasurski, the founder of the foreign press department, plus some hags—seven in all.

I didn't wait. I had nothing to lose. As if in a dream I walked in and picked up the slip of questions. Glanced at it. No, I certainly didn't know anything about the Communist media in Japan. And the question about the founding of the Bolshevik press in Siberia during the revolution didn't evoke any associations. General Kolchak? General Vrangel? Only these two names and also the two heroes thrown into the engine furnace, whatever they were called, knocked inside my poor empty head. But the Bolshevik press?

I stood up and walked over to the execution spot in front of the committee. The members were still fresh; it was early. In the middle sat our chair, with a prosthetic arm and eyes of different colors that also looked artificial. He wore the severe expression of a character in a horror movie. (The teachers in our department were famous for their fantastic appearance. One instructor, of dialectic materialism, barely cleared the edge of the table and sometimes lectured, invisible, from underneath it.)

There I was, standing at ease in front of the committee. I declared in a relaxed voice, not without some swagger: "I can't answer these questions."

The committee woke up and fidgeted excitedly. What an adventure! They politely suggested I try another ticket. I did.

"These questions I can't answer either. Any questions, in fact."

"Okay." The fellow on the far right fidgeted in alarm. "Tell us, what did Comrade Khrushchev call journalists?"

The plump lady in the middle sat back in her chair and moved her lips, prompting me. But I had no time for such details.

"Don't know," I announced proudly.

Everyone looked embarrassed. It began to look serious.

"Party executives!" the fellow said, reproaching me.

"Ah, right," I agreed, as though remembering.

Pause. No one knew when or how to kick me out. Terror filled the air. Behind me the elite forces of our class were straining their brains.

Surprising myself, I made a shocking announcement: "None of it will come in handy, you know."

Pause. They couldn't believe their ears. A graduate denounces her education within the very walls of her university.

"What exactly won't come in handy?" a fellow asked in a leading manner.

"All of it! Foreign press!"

Zasurski sat up straight. It was his life's work, the product of an enthusiastic polyglot!

"I'm going to the virgin lands in three days," I declared with all the force of a wholesome proletarian. "To work construction.

That's right. Because one needs to study life—before writing about it."

The committee grew wistful. Now they faced the problem of slinging an F at a future proletarian, whose thinking, incidentally, was ideologically sound. Damn Zasurski and his foreign press. What do these cretins need foreign press for? Who's ever going to read it? So what if it's Communist—it's all in foreign languages that no one knows. Hindi, Japanese—who can understand them? Communist, fine, but who can tell exactly what they write there?

They were probably thinking: One can send a failing student to cover some remote construction site for a year, to air her brain, but this one is actually volunteering! Lecturing us along the way, loudly and proudly.

These subtleties I didn't grasp at that moment, but in my five years of college I had firmly grasped the main demagogic principles. Virgin lands. Proletarian work for the benefit of common peasants, common workers. The committee must have sensed the classical Bolshevik connotations: the supremacy of the working class over the rotten intelligentsia; bringing culture to the people; potential letters to the Central Party Committee, God forbid. They all denounced each other.

This must have been the only way of talking to such people.

I retreated, chin high. Students listening at the door parted before me like the Red Sea. I crossed the hall, smiling belligerently. Then I found a little nook and hid there.

That's it, the end of the line, I thought miserably. I won't get a diploma, and no one will hire me, not a single provincial rag. We'll have nothing to live on, and next year I'll have to take the same exam over again. Damn you, Communist press of Japan.

Then there was a commotion in the hall, and we were summoned to hear our grades. I got a C! I laughed out loud from shock. That laughter rang sacrilegiously at the solemn moment of graduation.

The committee members were hiding their eyes, looking past me bitterly, like a multiheaded dragon who had let the rabbit slip across the river. It was clear that at that moment they would gladly slug me with an F. But that was spilled milk.

.   .   .

On graduation I had five rubles to my name, and I submitted them to the head of the student brigade. Buses carted us to the freight station. We climbed into cattle cars equipped with bunks, and I began to elaborate the plan for my future. I planned to work that summer with the students in northern Kazakhstan, and then, after they left, remain in the steppes and hitchhike from town to town toward the Pacific Ocean, writing for local papers along the way, the same route Chekhov once took. I would survive on fees from my writing and study the life of ordinary people. For some reason I considered that my most important goal.

This way I was keeping the promise I gave to the exam committee. I broke my back at the construction site, as a simple laborer, carrying stone blocks in 120-degree heat, without access to a shower (twice in two months), with saline drinking-water out of a barrel, without access to mail, with identical meals of brown pasta mixed with boiled lamb fat.

After a month of such life, we were covered with lice and

pimples, and even organized a strike of sorts: we sat listlessly around our grain silo like some displeased slaves at the unfinished Colosseum, and refused to work. This could have been interpreted as an economic crime and gotten us all expelled from the university and the Komsomol, but our leader, a math graduate student named Belenky, didn't think like that. He didn't care about ideology. He was simply a good person. Instead he borrowed a pickup truck and took us to the collective farm's public bath, and also gave us some money to buy candy and mailing supplies. We walked into the stationery store as if it were paradise. As soon as we were ready to leave, a squall flew in and an ocean of water descended on the steppe, which before our eyes turned into a green carpet of grass, and the road turned into a swamp. We were driving through runny mud in our truck, happy, filthy up to our eyebrows, singing songs.

After another week of this life I was discovered on the floor behind the oven in our stuffy barracks, burning with fever. The heads of the other brigades had driven from Bulaevo, the district center, specifically to find me: I was the only professional journalist in a territory three times the size of France. Looking at me politely, they offered me a change: to leave for Bulaevo and start working on the newsletter. At first I refused, considering it a betrayal; but two days later, when they came again, I agreed—things were winding down anyway—and quickly began to recover.

It was a fantastic life. Freedom. Endless spaces. I traveled from brigade to brigade, interviewing students, writing down anecdotes and songs. The only ones I never visited were the journalists: I had had my fill of my future colleagues.

I hitchhiked; rides were far apart. I had to wait for hours, lying in the grass under the faded blue sky, in the ringing emptiness. There is nothing more beautiful than the steppe. Nothing. Even the ocean is smaller and ends sooner. For the rest of my days I will remember the sunrise over the steppe: a recently plowed purple earth and an orange sun trembling over the horizon like an enormous egg yolk. On the road a truck stops, letting out milk women in white robes, colored red by the rising sun; the herd of cows arrives in waves, led by the mounted cowherds, who yell greetings at the women in German. The women, tall and healthy, incredibly clean and even starched, respond with laughter. They are ethnic Germans from the Volga region, exiled by Stalin to Kazakhstan.

When everyone returned to Moscow and I was ready to press ahead toward the Pacific, the informed people from the district paper warned me that local rags didn't pay freelancers and that permanent positions were filled with Party members—I wouldn't make enough money to rent a cot; plus no one would want to publish my pieces anyway. They were right about that: local media weren't interested in creativity. I looked through their archive: it was teeth-pulling misery. Local editors published cheerful news from collective farms—who harvested what crop ahead of whom; interviews with the farms' chairmen—and ideologically correct rubbish by the state news agency, themselves squeezed on all sides by the local Party organs, at the very bottom of the Party ocean. The farther you got from the capital, the center, the more conspicuous you became; there was too much empty space, no crowd to disappear in. I couldn't survive there.

That spring, before my graduation, I thought of another way of finding a job: through my estranged father. Stefan Petrushevsky was a professor of Marxist philosophy and a member of the editorial board of *Science and Religion*, a respected magazine. He could help. After a long search I discovered him in the same courtyard where I'd spent five years: his department was directly across from mine.

He knew about me. Rumors of my ideologically unsteady behavior had reached him. He seemed a little frightened and even jumped up when I walked into his office. Before that I had seen him exactly once, ten years earlier. Still, we recognized each other immediately: the call of blood, apparently. Recovering his nerve, he took me to a restaurant on the waterfront and bought me a meal. At the end he asked cautiously about my future plans. His tone told me that asking him for anything would be useless.

"I'm going to the virgin lands as a common laborer."

He seemed relieved: "That's how all careers take off!" He gave me ten rubles.

I visited him one more time, for no reason. Missed him, perhaps. He remarked: "My wife is against our meetings, but I told her, 'Who knows, she may be useful to me one day.'" Then he took me to the cafeteria. I never saw him again, my amazingly wise father.

This is the story preceding my appearance at the Petropavlovsk radio station.

The next day, after the editor's call I got off the local train (dragged by an ancient steam engine) and very soon sat in a warm, bright studio in front of the microphone, recapping my newsletter. Every piece was presented as a "novella." I also sang the brigade's work songs and played my guitar. I sang for no less than an hour, also performing some prison songs. For the Soviet radio it must have been a huge novelty.

As I was leaving the studio, in my duck bell-bottoms, tanned like a mulatto with hair faded to bone white, my whole appearance beyond exotic, I was approached by a well-groomed gentleman of about forty.

"Where does a character like you come from?" he inquired politely.

"Bulaevo, that's where."

"Where is that?"

"Thirty-five miles from here."

"How interesting. My name is Konstantin Ardi. I work at *The Late Night News*."

From the far corner another old fellow of about thirty-five nodded. He looked fatigued in the extreme. That's how people look the morning after a major binge. I had completed an internship at Gorky's local paper, among the hard-drinking local correspondents, and could tell different shades of hangover.

"And this is Vasily Ananchenko. We came together. We really liked you."

Vasily attempted a smile. His eyes were the same purple color as the bags underneath. He crossed his legs and drooped again.

Young girls react with caution when greeted with compliments by middle-aged strangers. I pricked my ears.

"If only you were a Muscovite," Ardi declared, "we would have hired you for our program!"

"I am a Muscovite," I replied sternly.

My 1960s.

A heavy pause followed. A promise was made.

"Well, here's the phone number," Ardi said, recovering courteously. "My wife, Alexandra Ilyina, is the head of the arts and culture section." Aha, "my wife."

The editor who had invited me to Petropavlovsk interrupted us and took me home, where his wife fed me dumplings and then entertained me with stories about their life in Petropavlovsk, which they called "Petroholesk."

The children ran around me wildly, and then I was assigned a little room with two featherbeds. The moment I sank into their luxurious softness I was attacked by an army of bedbugs, eager to taste new blood. Poor us, how we all lived.

I finished printing the newsletter and brought the copies with me to Moscow. I stayed at home for a month amidst my mother's moaning that we couldn't survive on her salary, which was true—mothers always inform their children of the unpleasant truths they refuse to recognize. Then I gathered my nerve and dialed the number.

"Where on earth are you?" a smoky female basso replied. It was Ms. Ilyina, Ardi's wife. "We've been waiting and waiting. Ardi told me all about you."

I arrived at the radio station, received an assignment to cover the return of the student brigades, as if it had just happened instead of happening two months before, then handed in my report to Ilyina. She read it, nodded, and sent me to the recording studio. That same night, sitting at our radio head to head, Mama and I listened to my very first radio appearance. What a squeaky,

The photograph on my first work ID, at the radio station, in 1962.

shrill voice! I couldn't understand a word. I sounded like I was chewing something.

Nonetheless, I began working there part-time.

Two months later, Ilyina gave me a full-time position.

My wise father was right, after all. My adult life took off in the steppes, on a Socialist construction site, just as he had predicted . . .

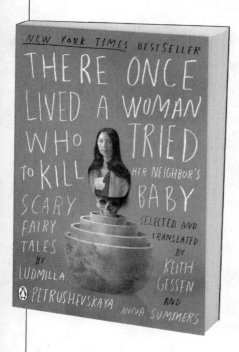

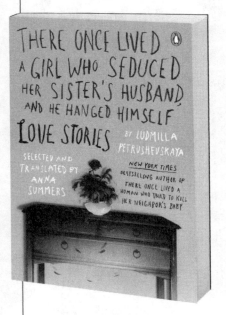